Alastair Sawday's

Special Places to Stay

The Cotswolds

First edition
Copyright © 2010 Alastair Sawday
Publishing Co. Ltd

Published in May 2010

Alastair Sawday Publishing Co. Ltd,
The Old Farmyard, Yanley Lane,
Long Ashton, Bristol BS41 9LR, UK
Tel: +44 (0)1275 395430
Fax: +44 (0)1275 393388
Email: info@sawdays.co.uk
Web: www.sawdays.co.uk

The Globe Pequot Press,
P. O. Box 480, Guilford,
Connecticut 06437, USA
Tel: +1 203 458 4500
Fax: +1 203 458 4601
Email: info@globepequot.com
Web: www.globepequot.com

Maps: Maidenhead Cartographic Services
Printing: Butler, Tanner & Dennis
UK distribution: Penguin UK, London

ISBN-13: 978-1-906136-48-2

Alastair Sawday has asserted his right to
be identified as the author of this work.

*We have made every effort to ensure the
accuracy of the information in this book at
the time of going to press. However, we cannot
accept any responsibility for any loss, injury
or inconvenience resulting from the use of
information contained therein.*

Cover design: Company X, Bristol.
Cover photo credits. Thanks to:
1. Getty Images/Barbara Van Zanten 2. istock.com 3. Getty Images/Peter Anderson
Photo right: istock.com

Contents

The buildings

Beautiful as they were, our old offices leaked heat, used electricity to heat water and rooms, flooded spaces with light to illuminate one person, and were not ours to alter. So in 2005 we created our own eco-offices by converting some old barns to create a low-emissions building. We made the building energy-efficient through a variety of innovative and energy-saving building techniques, described below.

Insulation We went to great lengths to ensure that very little heat will escape, by:
• laying insulating board 90mm thick immediately under the roof tiles and on the floor
• lining the whole of the inside of the building with plastic sheeting to ensure air-tightness
• fixing further insulation underneath the roof and between the rafters
• fixing insulated plaster-board to add yet another layer of insulation.
All this means we are insulated for the Arctic, and almost totally air-tight.

Heating We installed a wood-pellet boiler from Austria, in order to be largely fossil-fuel free. The pellets are made from compressed sawdust, a waste product from timber mills that work only with sustainably managed forests. The heat is conveyed by water, throughout the building, via an under-floor system.

Water We installed a 6000-litre tank to collect rainwater from the roofs. This is pumped back, via an ultra-violet filter, to the lavatories, showers and basins. There are two solar thermal panels on the roof providing heat to the one (massively insulated) hot-water cylinder.

Lighting We have a carefully planned mix of low-energy lighting: task lighting and up-lighting. We also installed three sun-pipes – polished aluminium tubes that reflect the outside light down to chosen areas of the building.

Electricity All our electricity has long come from the Good Energy company and is 100% renewable.

Materials Virtually all materials are non-toxic or natural. Our carpets, for example, are made from (80%) Herdwick sheep-wool from National Trust farms in the Lake District.

Doors and windows Outside doors and new windows are wooden, double-glazed and beautifully constructed in Norway. Old windows have been double-glazed.

We have a building we are proud of, and architects and designers are fascinated by. But best of all, we are now in a better position to encourage our owners and readers to take sustainability more seriously.

What we do

Besides having moved the business to a low-carbon building, the company works in a number of ways to reduce its overall environmental footprint.

Our footprint We measure our footprint annually and use this information to find ways of reducing our environmental impact. To help address unavoidable carbon emissions

we try to put something back: since 2006 we have supported SCAD, an organisation that works with villagers in India to create genuinely sustainable development.

Our office Nearly all of our office waste is recycled; kitchen waste is composted and used in the office vegetable garden. Left-over fruit and veg goes to the locally-owned pigs across the lane, who have recently been joined by chickens rescued from battery farms. Organic and fairtrade basic provisions are used in the staff kitchen and at in-house events, and green cleaning products are used throughout the office.

Photo: Tom Germain

For many years we have been 'greening' the business in different ways. Our aim is to reduce our environmental footprint as far as possible, and almost every decision we make takes into account the environmental implications. In recognition of our efforts we won a Business Commitment to the Environment Award in 2005, and in 2006 a Queen's Award for Enterprise in the Sustainable Development category. In that year Alastair was voted ITN's 'Eco Hero'. In 2009 we were given the South West C+ Carbon Positive Consumer Choices Award for our Ethical Collection.

In 2008 and again in 2009 we won the IPG Environmental Award. In 2009 we were also the IPG overall Independent Publisher and Trade Publisher of the Year. The judging panel were effusive in their praise, stating: "With green issues currently at the forefront of publishers' minds, Alastair Sawday Publishing was singled out in this category as a model for all independents to follow. Its efforts to reduce waste in its office and supply chain have reduced the company's environmental impact, and it works closely with staff to identify more areas of improvement. Here is a publisher who lives and breathes green. Alastair Sawday has all the right principles and is clearly committed to improving its practice further."

We don't plan to pursue growth for growth's sake. The Sawday's name – and thus our future – depends on maintaining our integrity. We promote special places – those that add beauty, authenticity and a touch of humanity to our lives. This is a niche, albeit a growing one, so we will spend time pursuing truly special places rather than chasing the mass market.

That said, we do plan to produce more titles as well as to diversify. We are explanding our Go Slow series and have published *Green Europe*, both projects designed to raise the profile of low-impact tourism. Our Fragile Earth imprint is a collection of campaigning books about the environment that will keep you up to date and well-armed for the battle with apathy.

The Cotswold escarpment creeps into Wiltshire and Oxford, though few of us would argue with the less geological view of the Cotswolds belonging to Gloucestershire. And fewer of us would dispute their ravishing beauty. That beauty is deeply engrained in the British psyche as inalienable, inevitable, indestructible. I hope it is.

We have chosen to do this regional guide because it, too, was inevitable. We are connected to so many handsome buildings – pubs, B&Bs, hotels and holiday homes – in the Cotswolds that we wanted to bring them under one roof. We are immensely proud of them, and they in their turn are proud of their Cotswolds – with good reason.

The *Shell Guide of 1980* introduced the Cotswolds charmingly: "We know we are in the Cotswolds when the houses are built of limestone and the fields are divided by drystone walls rather than hedges; fields which are smooth and sculptured, and stone which catches every change of light

Photo: Tom Germain

and grows mosses green as cress, and lichens varying from bright rust to black that turn yellow-green to an intricately textured white; good country for sheep and barley."

My own Cotswold memories are of beech avenues dappling the sun as it beat down over nearby cornfields of rich golden hue, of constant delight at the stone-yellow houses and the villages that seem to have defied the industrial world. I remember the stiles built of stone, the great upright stones on the tops of the walls and their delightful name: 'cock-ups'. The village names roll easily off the tongue: Birdlip, Lechlade, Bourton-on-the-Water, Burford, Milton under Wychwood. We all know them, but should go to see them too, for there is fascination at every turn.

There are countless little valleys, undulating hillsides – though never very high – burbling streams such as the famous Windrush, and woods to walk in rather than stare at. No great conifer plantations here, just well-managed acres. The land once teemed with sheep, which gave the area much of its wealth. Now the farming is more mixed. Perhaps the continuing existence of some great estates also adds beauty, for there is money to do the right thing.

It is fine country for walking and cycling, with tiny roads cut deep into the landscape by time and weather, unravelling to unexpected places and muddling in their mellow profusion. But it is fine country just to be in, with almost every corner revealing its own version of the famous Cotswold beauty. These beautiful Special Places to stay (and drink) are the icing on a very rich cake.

Alastair Sawday

Photo right: Sequoia House, entry 98
Photo left: Sherborne Forge, entry 46

It's simple. There are no rules, no boxes to tick. We choose places that we like and are fiercely subjective in our choices. We also recognise that one person's idea of special is not necessarily someone else's so there is a huge variety of places, and prices, in the book. Those who are familiar with our Special Places series know that we look for comfort, originality, authenticity, and reject the insincere, the anonymous and the banal. The way guests are treated comes as high on our list as the setting, the architecture, the atmosphere and the food.

Inspections

We visit every place in the guide to get a feel for how both house and owner tick. We don't take a clipboard and we don't have a list of what is acceptable and what is not. Instead, we chat for an hour or so with the owner or manager and look round. It's all very informal, but it gives us an excellent idea of who would enjoy staying there. If the visit happens to be the last of the day, we sometimes stay the night. Once in the book,

properties are re-inspected every few years so that we can keep things fresh and accurate.

Feedback

In between inspections we rely on feedback from our army of readers, as well as from staff members who are encouraged to visit properties across the series. This feedback is invaluable to us and we always follow up on comments.

So do tell us whether your stay has been a joy or not, if the atmosphere was great or stuffy, the owners and staff cheery or bored. The accuracy of the book depends on what you, and our inspectors, tell us. A lot of the new entries in each edition are recommended by our readers, so keep telling us about new places you've discovered too. Please use the forms on our website at www.sawdays.co.uk, or later in this book (page 151).

However, please do not tell us if your starter was cold or the bedside light broken – tell the owner, immediately, and get them to do something about it. Most owners, and staff, are more than happy to correct problems and will bend over backwards to help. Far better than bottling it up and then writing to us a week later!

Subscriptions

Owners pay to appear in our guides. Their fees go towards the high costs of inspecting, of producing an all-colour book and of maintaining our website. We only include places and owners that we find positively special. It is not possible for anyone to buy their way into our guides.

Disclaimer

We make no claims to pure objectivity in choosing these places. They are here simply because we like them. Our opinions and tastes are ours alone and this book is a statement of them; we hope you will share them. We have done our utmost to get our facts right but apologise unreservedly for any mistakes that may have crept in. The latest information we have about each place can be found on our website, www.sawdays.co.uk.

Photo right: Old Manor Cottage, entry 91

You should know that we don't check such things as fire regulations, swimming pool security or any other laws with which owners of properties receiving paying guests should comply. This is the responsibility of the owners.

Finding the right place for you

Our descriptions are carefully written to help you steer clear of places that will not suit you, but lead you instead to personal paradise. So read between the lines: what we don't say is sometimes as important as what we do.

Wherever you choose to stay, remember that the owners are experts at knowing their patch. They can often recommend secret beaches, excellent restaurants, super walks and gardens to visit – occasionally ones that aren't usually open to the public. Some places may provide maps and a bus timetable; some owners may be happy to pick you up at the end of a long walk. Do ask.

On the B&B pages you will find a huge variety of places, and also owners: some will be hovering with freshly baked cake when you arrive, others may be out shopping for your supper, having left a key under a stone. Mostly these are people's homes; you will encounter family life and its attendant chaos in some, and complete privacy in others, while a fair number of owners will be happy for you to stay all day.

For those who prefer more anonymity, there are many wonderful hotels, some child-friendly, others more suited to those who prefer peace and quiet. A sprinkling of deeply spoiling hotels will keep the fashionistas happy, while there are family-run and comfortably old-fashioned places for traditionalists. There are also gorgeous self-catering places, some classically contemporary, a few crisply chic, many simple but cosy. Choose from dreamy wilderness boltholes for two, sweet cottages for families, or magnificent houses for larger gatherings.

Maps & directions

Each property is flagged with its entry number on the maps at the front. These maps are the best start to planning your trip, but you'll need a proper road map for real navigation. Most places will send you detailed instructions once you have booked your stay.

Photo : The Cockloft, Sheldon Manor, entry 105

Symbols

Below each entry you will see some symbols, which are explained at the very back of the book. They are based on information given to us by owners. However, things do change: bikes may be under repair or WiFi may have been added. Please use the symbols as a guide rather than an absolute statement of fact. Owners occasionally bend their own rules, so it is worth asking if you may take your child or dog, even if the entry doesn't have the symbol.

Children – The ⚭ symbol is given to owners who accept children of any age. It does not mean they will necessarily have cots, highchairs, safety equipment etc, so do check. If an owner welcomes children but only those above a certain age, this is stated at the end of the description. Even these folk may accept your younger child if you are the only guests. Many who say no to children do so not because they don't like them but because they may have a steep stair, an unfenced pond or they find balancing the needs of mixed age groups too challenging.

Pets – The 🐕 symbol is given to places where your pet can sleep in your bedroom but not on the bed. Be realistic about your pet – if it is nervous or excitable or doesn't like the company of other dogs, people, chickens or children, then say so.

Photo left: Church Farm Cottage, entry 107
Photo right: Sandpipers, entry 22

Rooms

We tell you if bedrooms are doubles, twin/double (ie. with zip and link beds), suite (with a sitting area), family or single. Most owners are flexible and can often juggle beds or bedrooms; talk to them about what you need before you book. Most bedrooms in our B&Bs and hotels have an en suite bath or shower room; we only mention bathroom details when they do not. Please check with owners for bathroom details for self-catering places.

Meals

In B&Bs and hotels a full cooked breakfast is included in the room price, unless we say otherwise.

Obviously if you have chosen to self-cater, you must organise your own. Many of our hotels offer a half-board option, and some of our B&Bs will arrange an evening meal on request.

Bookings and cancellations

Requests for deposits vary; some are non-refundable, and some owners may charge you for the whole of the booked stay in advance.

Some cancellation policies are also more stringent than others. Some will charge you the total cost if you cancel at short notice. If they hold your credit card details they may deduct a cancellation fee from it and not contact you to discuss this. So ask owners to explain their cancellation policy clearly before booking so you understand exactly where you stand; it may well help you avoid a nasty surprise.

Payment

All our owners take cash and UK cheques with a cheque card. Those who also take credit cards have the appropriate symbol.

Photo: Clapton Manor, entry 103

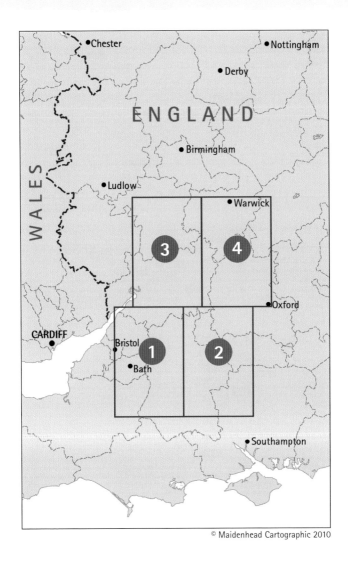

© Maidenhead Cartographic 2010

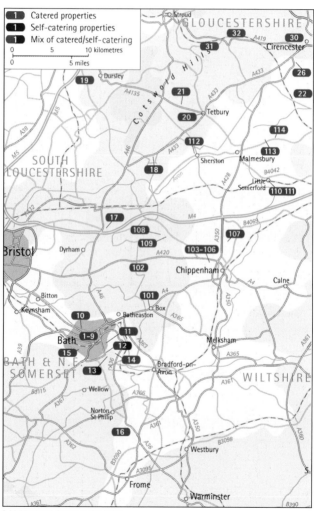

© Maidenhead Cartographic 2010

Map 2

19

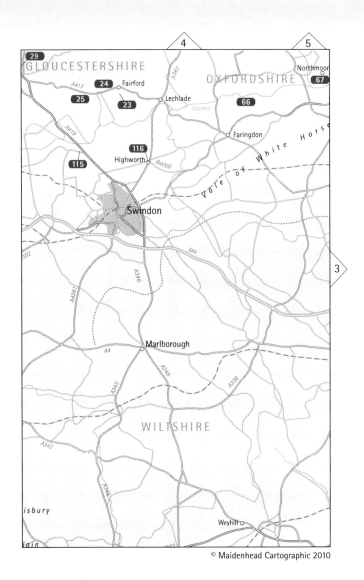

© Maidenhead Cartographic 2010

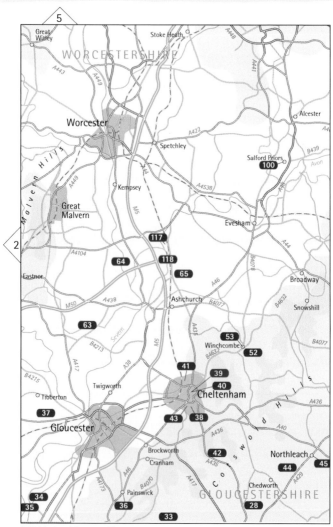

© Maidenhead Cartographic 2010

Map 4

21

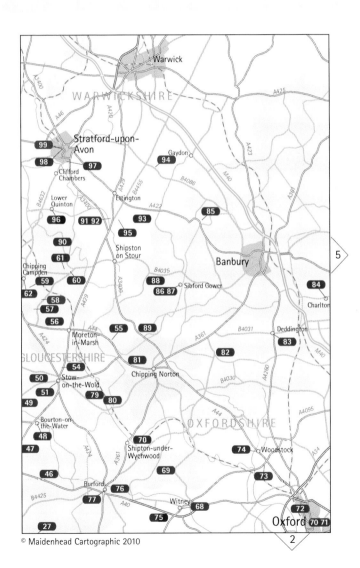

The Cotswolds

SACO Serviced Apartments, Bath

Wander fabulous Bath's streets for elegant squares, pavement cafés, delicious delis and the Roman Baths (there's a spa if you want to take a dip). Close to the river, in the middle of town, these serviced apartments bask behind a beautifully restored Regency façade – look out for the pillared entrances. Inside is a collection of airy studios and apartments, some small, some big, all with white walls, Italian designer furniture, sparkling kitchens, flat-screen TVs, CD players and big fluffy towels. There's a lift to whisk you up and away, 24-hour reception, and broadband throughout. *Minimum stay two nights at weekends.*

Price	Studios: £63–£135; 1-bed apt: £138–£172; 2-bed apt: £236–£278.
Rooms	43 studios & apartments for 2 & 4.
Meals	Full kitchen facilities. Restaurants within 0.5 miles.
Closed	Never.
Directions	In centre of town, 5-minute walk from station. Full directions on booking.

Sean Mason
31–40 St James's Parade, Bath BA1 1UH

Tel	+44 (0)1225 486540
Web	bath.sacoapartments.co.uk

The Queensberry Hotel & Olive Tree Restaurant

Three grand houses, built by John Wood in 1771, in the architectural epicentre of Bath. Grand first-floor rooms are some of the best in town, while high ceilings, magnificent windows and Georgian colours run throughout. The four-poster comes in ivory white (with a chaise longue in the bathroom), but all rooms are luxurious, including the smallest up in the eaves. Downstairs are flowers in the sitting room, a fire in the bar and contemporary art in the candlelit restaurant where super food waits: delicious duck, perfect venison, fabulous poached figs. Staff are delightful, too. *Minimum stay two nights at weekends.*

Price	£115–£230. Suites £235–£450.
Rooms	29: 26 twins/doubles, 1 four-poster, 2 suites.
Meals	Breakfast £10–£15. Lunch £16.50. Dinner, à la carte, about £38.
Closed	Never.
Directions	Into Bath on A4 London Rd to Paragon; 1st right into Lansdown; 2nd left into Bennett St; 1st right into Russel St.

Laurence & Helen Beere
Russel Street, Bath BA1 2QF

Tel   +44 (0)1225 447928
Web   www.thequeensberry.co.uk

Entry 2 Map 1

77 Great Pulteney Street

Tea and cakes await down the elegant stone steps to a garden flat in this broad street of immaculate Georgian houses. Inside all is pale wood, modern art, bergère chairs and palms. Downstairs is a comfortable bedroom with loads of books and its own door to a small but delightfully well-designed garden. On fine days you breakfast here without haste, on fruit from Ian and Henry's allotment, and gorgeous bacon and sausage butties; Ian is a fanatic foodie and dinner will also be special, but there are lots of good places to eat – and shop – nearby. Henry may play the Northumbrian pipes for you if you ask nicely…

Price	£75-£95. Singles from £55.
Rooms	1 double.
Meals	Dinner from £20. Packed lunch from £5.
Closed	Rarely.
Directions	A4 into centre of Bath. Last house before Laura Place on south side of Great Pulteney St. Parking by arrangement; 7-minute walk from station.

Ian Critchley & Henry Ford
Bath BA2 4DL
Tel   +44 (0)1225 466659
Web   www.77pulteneyst.co.uk

Bathwick Gardens

The period, hand-printed wallpaper is just one of the remarkable features of this elegant Grade I-listed house: Julian is an expert. The house, in one of Bath's finest Regency terraces, has been so beautifully restored that the BBC used its rooms for Jane Austen's *Persuasion*. Bedrooms are flooded with light and views are stunning; one stylish bathroom has marquina marble, cherrywood and ebony. Breakfast is taken in the family kitchen, or in the conservatory. For the adventurous, Mechthild serves up an Austrian alternative of cold meats and cheeses, fresh rye breads and homemade cakes. Herrlich!

Price	£95–£120. Singles £85.
Rooms	3 twins/doubles.
Meals	Pub/restaurant 300 yds.
Closed	Rarely.
Directions	A46 to Rath, then A4 for city centre. Left onto A36 over Cleveland Bridge; follow signs to Holburne Museum. Directly after museum, left. House on right.

Mechthild Self von Hippel
95 Sydney Place, Bath BA2 6NE

Tel	+44 (0)1225 469435
Web	www.bathwickgardens.co.uk

14 Raby Place

A listed Regency house within walking distance of one of Europe's most beautiful cities. Muriel likes modern art and has filled the elegant rooms with stunning pictures and objects, antique chairs and lovely fabrics. Beautifully proportioned double bedrooms are graceful and spotless with laundered linen; one on the top (third) floor has fabulous views over the city to the Abbey, the smaller single has a piano in case you get the urge. Breakfast is organic, delicious, and eaten at a communal table in the dining room; chat to Muriel or bury your head in a paper.
Free parking permit for road outside.

Price	£65–£70. Singles £35.
Rooms	5: 2 doubles, 1 family room; 1 twin with separate shower; 1 single with separate bath. (Cot available.)
Meals	Restaurants 8-minute walk.
Closed	Never.
Directions	Bathwick Hill is turning off A36 towards Bristol; look for signs to university. No. 14 on left-hand side as you go uphill, before left turn into Raby Mews.

Muriel Guy
Bathwick, Bath BA2 4EH

Tel +44 (0)1225 465120

Entry 5 Map 1

The Bath Courtyard

You are a brisk ten-minute walk from the centre, but all is hushed in this Bath stone cottage, neatly tucked down a back lane. Shoes must be removed at the door; pad through to a dining room with a big mahogany table and interesting paintings, a large conservatory for breakfasts (fresh fruit salad, smoked salmon and scrambled eggs) and a long, rose-filled garden. Bedrooms are perfectly presented in pale yellows, with silk curtains, pocket-sprung mattresses and well-lit, ultra-modern bathrooms. Borrow bikes from Michael and his partner, and head for the tow path, or pedal into town for the shops and sights.

Price	£90–£110. Singles £75.
Rooms	2 doubles.
Meals	Pubs/restaurants 0.25 miles.
Closed	Rarely.
Directions	M4, Bath signs; London Road, over river (Cleveland Bridge), past fire station. Right at next lights; left into Sydney Place; Vellore Lane 200 yds on right. Private parking is available.

Michael Wilson
38 Vellore Lane, Bath BA2 6JQ

Tel   +44 (0)1225 424741
Web   www.thebathcourtyard.co.uk

Tolley Cottage

Breakfast on the patio on fine days and watch the barges pass the bottom of the gorgeous garden; raise your eyes to Bath Abbey on the skyline. This Victorian house is a ten-minute walk from city centre, spa and fine Georgian theatre. Sunny and bright, rooms are a comfortable mix of contemporary and classical; books, art and interesting glass pieces catch the eye. Bedrooms are small, calming and charming with elegant furnishings and long views; bathrooms sparkle. Judy does outstanding breakfasts; James, Master of Wine, can arrange tastings. Both are warm and relaxed, and love sharing their home.

Price	From £100. Singles from £90.
Rooms	2: 1 double, 1 twin.
Meals	Pubs/restaurants 10-minute walk.
Closed	Christmas.
Directions	Follow signs for American Museum & University up Bathwick Hill. Take 1st turn right to Sydney Buildings. House 200 yds on right. Free parking.

Judy & James John
23 Sydney Buildings, Bath BA2 6BZ

Tel	+44 (0)1225 463365
Web	www.tolleycottage.co.uk

Bath Paradise House Hotel

The views draw you out as soon as you enter: a magical advertisement for this World Heritage city. Nearly all the rooms make full use of the view; the best have bay windows, two are in the garden extension, all have a soft, luxurious country feel with contemporary fabrics and fabulous bathrooms. The sitting room's stone-arched French windows pull in the light, the staff are lovely and all is relaxed. Don't miss afternoon tea in a half-acre walled garden: you'll lose yourself in the vista. The occasional peal of bells comes for a nearby church, and Thermae Bath Spa is a must. *Seven-minute walk down hill to centre.*

Price	£75–£175. Singles £65–£115.
Rooms	11: 4 doubles, 3 twins, 1 family room, 3 four-posters.
Meals	Restaurants in Bath half a mile.
Closed	24 & 25 December.
Directions	From train station one-way system to Churchill Bridge. A367 exit from r'bout up hill; 0.75 miles, left at Andrews estate agents. Left down hill into cul-de-sac; on left.

David & Annie Lanz
86–88 Holloway, Bath BA2 4PX

Tel	+44 (0)1225 317723
Web	www.paradise-house.co.uk

Entry 8 Map 1

Dorian House

A Victorian townhouse owned by a musician with a love of interior design. Step into a tiled hallway with exquisite stained glass, sink into the sitting room's sofas or pop a bottle of champagne in super bedrooms named after cellists. The most impressive, and the most secluded, is du Pré, its huge four-poster bed reached up a flight of stairs. Every room is decorated with beautiful fabrics, interesting art and Egyptian linen; those on the first floor are traditional, those above have a funkier feel, three have fabulous marble bathrooms. Relaxation assured, and wonderful breakfasts. *Minimum stay two nights at weekends.*

Price	£80-£160. Singles £60-£89.
Rooms	11: 3 twins/doubles, 4 doubles, 1 family room, 3 four-posters.
Meals	Pubs & restaurants within walking distance.
Closed	Never.
Directions	From Bath centre, follow signs to Shepton Mallet to sausage-shaped r'bout, then A37 up hill, 1st right. House 3rd on left, signed.

Kathryn & Tim Hugh
One Upper Oldfield Park, Bath BA2 3JX

Tel	+44 (0)1225 426336
Web	www.dorianhouse.co.uk

The Bath Priory Hotel, Restaurant & Spa

The Bath Priory is hotel heaven: everything is exquisite. Staff welcome you by name, the drawing room doubles as an art gallery, a four-acre garden comes with croquet lawn and swimming pool. Burn off a few calories in the spa, then return for something ambrosial from a Michelin-starred kitchen. Bedrooms are matchless, with rich fabrics, warm colours, fine wallpaper, shelves of books; beds are turned down while you're at dinner. Bathrooms are impeccable (one has fossils embedded in Jura stone). As for the city, stroll through the park to the Roman Baths and the peerless Royal Crescent. *Minimum stay two nights at weekends.*

Price	£260–£410. Suites £495–£595.
Rooms	31 twins/doubles.
Meals	Lunch from £24. Dinner £65. Tasting menu £90.
Closed	Never.
Directions	From centre of Bath follow red hospital signs west for a mile. Right at far end of Royal Victoria Park. Left at T-junction into Weston Road. Hotel on left.

Sue Williams
Weston Road, Bath BA1 2XT

Tel	+44 (0)1225 331922
Web	www.thebathpriory.co.uk

Allens Cottage

The setting is exceptional: a 15-minute walk (uphill) from Bath, yet next door to Capability Brown-designed Prior Park, with woodland, grottos and an ornamental Palladian bridge (one of four in the world!). The cottage is just as good, combining a cosy feel with modern touches. Three charming bedrooms share a roomy bathroom; downstairs, a modern kitchen and a table for six, and a sitting room you'd wish was your own. There are two gardens and a sun terrace (watch young children, there are some steep drops). Nearby there's the White Hart for delicious meals and the owners live right next door. *Free entry to Prior Park.*

Price	£820–£1,300 per week.
Rooms	Cottage for 6: 2 doubles, 1 twin, bathroom & shower room.
Meals	Self-catering.
Closed	Rarely.
Directions	Given on booking.

Roger & Alex Chapman
Church Lane, Widcombe, Bath BA2 6BD

Tel	+44 (0)1225 830062
Web	www.bathcitycottages.co.uk

Entry 11 Map 1

55a North Road

Prepare yourself for a surprise. A short hop from Capability Brown-designed Prior Park, hidden down a narrow drive off one of Bath's less remarkable streets, is an architectural novelty – only the roof tiles give away the 1980s origins. Energetic owners Natalie and Guy offer you two completely private self-contained studios each with its own entrance, small kitchen and comfy chairs. Find a mix of ultra-modern and traditional: newly laid oak floors or new carpets, limestone tiles in the bathrooms, wall-mounted flat screen TVs, old Irish bedheads and pure cotton linen. Natalie will bring a delicious breakfast to your room.

Price	From £100.
Rooms	2: 1 double, 1 twin.
Meals	Pubs/restaurants within 1 mile.
Closed	Rarely.
Directions	Turn off North Road in Combe Down between (and on same side as) Farrs Lane and Hadley Road into wide driveway. Keep left. 55a is behind number 55.

Natalie & Guy Woods
Combe Down, Bath BA2 5DF

Tel +44 (0)1225 835593
Web www.55anorthroad.co.uk

Grey Lodge

In a conservation area, yet only a short drive from the centre of Bath, the views are breathtaking from wherever you stand. The steep valley rolls out ahead of you from most of the rooms, and from the garden comes a confusion and a profusion of scents and colours – a glory in its own right. The friendly and likeable Sticklands are conservationists as well as gardeners and have a Green Certificate to prove it. Breakfasts are a feast: bacon and eggs, cereals, home-grown jam, smoked fish and much more. Jane will tell you all about wonderful local gardens to visit. *Self-catering apartment for four.*

Price	£80–£90. Singles £50–£55.
Rooms	3: 2 twins/doubles, 1 family room.
Meals	Pubs/restaurants 2 miles.
Closed	Rarely.
Directions	From A36, 3 miles out of Bath on Warminster road, take uphill road by lights & viaduct. 1st left, 100 yds, signed Monkton Combe. After village, house 1st on left; 0.5 miles on.

Jane & Anthony Stickland
Summer Lane, Combe Down, Bath BA2 7EU

Tel	+44 (0)1225 832069
Web	www.greylodge.co.uk

Entry 13 Map 1

Wheelwrights Arms

A pub for all seasons. In winter, grab the table in front of the fire where the wheelwright worked his magic; in summer, enjoy a pint on the terrace. Inside, beautiful colours mix with soft stone walls and timber frames. Logs are piled in the alcoves, there's a lovely snug and the food is delicious. Airy bedrooms in what was the wheelwright's annexe come in original style. Expect dark wood floors, shuttered windows, old-style radiators, flat-screen TVs. The inn holds two season tickets for Bath Rugby Club – at cost price, so book early – and the bus into Bath runs outside. *Minimum stay two nights at weekends.*

Price	£100–£145. Singles from £80.
Rooms	7: 5 doubles, 1 twin, 1 single.
Meals	Lunch, 2 courses, £10. Sunday lunch £11.50.
	Dinner, 3 courses, about £25.
Closed	Never.
Directions	A36 south from Bath for 3 miles, then right, signed
	Monkton Combe. Over x-roads, into village, on left.

David Phillips-White
Church Lane, Monkton Combe, Bath BA2 7HB
Tel   +44 (0)1225 722287
Web   www.wheelwrightsarms.co.uk

Entry 14 Map 1

Manor Farm Barn

Duchy of Cornwall farmland stretches as far as the eye can see; the views from this converted barn – with light open-plan spaces – are splendid by any standards, but remarkable considering you are so close to Bath. There's much wildlife, too: sparrowhawks nest in the gable end, buzzards circle above the valley, and deer may gaze at you eating your breakfast. Giles, who pots, and Sue, who paints, are gentle and easy-going hosts; spruce guest rooms have built-in wardrobes, houseplants and excellent beds. For those in search of birdsong and country peace after a day on the hoof in Bath.

Price	£80. Singles £40-£50.
Rooms	2: 1 twin/double; 1 double with separate shower.
Meals	Pubs/restaurants 2.5 miles.
Closed	Christmas & New Year.
Directions	From Bath, A367 (Wells Rd). At Red Lion r'bout right (Bristol A4). Straight on, pass Culverhay School on left. After 100 yds left to Englishcombe. There, right after postbox to church, fork right, follow road; last on right.

	Sue & Giles Barber
	Englishcombe, Bath BA2 9DU
Tel	+44 (0)1225 424195
Web	www.manorfarmbarn.com

Hollytree Cottage

Meandering lanes lead to this 16th-century cottage, with roses round the door, a grandfather clock in the hall and an air of genteel tranquillity. The cottage charm has been updated with Regency mahogany and sumptuous sofas. The bedrooms have views over undulating countryside; pretty bathrooms have oils, lotions and dove soaps in china dishes. Breakfast is in the lovely garden room looking onto hollyhocks in summer; the garden is sloping and sunny with a pond and some rare trees and shrubs. A place to come for absolute peace, birdsong and walks; the joys of elegant Bath is 20 minutes away and Julia can help you plan trips.

Price	£80–£90. Singles £45–£50.
Rooms	3: 1 double, 1 twin, 1 four-poster.
Meals	Pub/restaurant 0.5 miles.
Closed	Rarely.
Directions	From Bath, A36 to Wolverton. Just past Red Lion, turn for Laverton. 1 mile to x-roads; towards Faukland; downhill for 80 yds. On left, just above farm entrance on right.

Julia Naismith
Laverton, Bath BA2 7QZ
Tel +44 (0)1373 830786
Web www.hollytreecottagebath.co.uk

Little Smithy

Just minutes from the M4, the farming village is fairly quiet and your little cottage with mullioned windows completely private. Your front door opens into a hallway which runs the length of the building: at one end the creamy twin with bright red bedspreads and sparkling bathroom next door, and the other your L-shaped sitting room with an electric wood-burner. Upstairs is the comfy double and another smart bathroom; all is as neat as a pin. Joanna gives you breakfast in the main house, or on warm days in the garden: eggs from next door's hens, homemade bread and marmalade. Right on the Cotswold Way so perfect for walkers.

Price	£75. Singles £60.
Rooms	2 doubles.
Meals	Pub/restaurant 1 mile.
Closed	Christmas & Easter.
Directions	Bath A46 north. Cross M4 signed Stroud then almost immed. take 1st turning on right. After Compass Inn, 2nd turning on right into village. Past church; house first on right after left hand bend.

	Joanna Bowman
	Tormarton, Badminton GL9 1HU
Tel	+44 (0)1454 218412
Web	www.littlesmithy.com

Entry 17 Map 1

The King's Arms Inn

The roadside village inn sports slate floors, oak settles in the bar, and a cheekily bright front room adorned with lithographs of the area. In the dining room are terracotta walls, chunky wooden tables and high-backed chairs. There's a big fireplace for winter, darts and dominoes, a walled garden for summer, delicious daily-changing menus and a sign that reads, 'If they don't serve beer in heaven, then I'm not going'. Rooms upstairs, the quietest at the back, are cosy and inviting, with colourful throws on comfortable beds and spotless shower rooms; the self-catering cottages are in the coaching stable.

Price	£75. Single from £55. Cottages from £90.
Rooms	4 + 3: 1 double, 2 twins/doubles, 1 single. 3 self-catering cottages (2 for 4, 1 for 6).
Meals	Main courses £8.95-£16.95; bar meals £4.95-£9.95
Closed	Never.
Directions	M4 junc. 18, A46 north, then A433 for Tetbury. In village on left.

Alastair & Sarah Sadler
The Street, Didmarton, Badminton GL9 1DT
Tel   +44 (0)1454 238245
Web   www.kingsarmsdidmarton.co.uk

Drakestone House

A treat by anyone's reckoning. Utterly delightful people with wide-ranging interests (ex British Council and college lecturing; arts, travel, gardening) in a manor-type house full of beautiful furniture. The house was born of the Arts and Crafts movement: wooden panels painted green, a log-fired drawing room for guests, handsome old furniture, comfortable proportions, good beds with proper blankets. The garden's massive clipped hedges, Monterey Pines and smooth, great lawn are impressive, as is the whole place – and the views stretch to the Severn Estuary and Wales.

Price	£78. Singles £49.
Rooms	3: 1 twin/double, 1 double, 1 twin, all with separate bath/shower.
Meals	Dinner £32. BYO. Pub/restaurant under 1 mile.
Closed	Christmas.
Directions	B4060 from Stinchcombe to Wotton-under-Edge. 0.25 miles out of Stinchcombe village. Driveway on left marked, before long bend.

Hugh & Crystal Mildmay
Stinchcombe, Dursley GL11 6AS

Tel   +44 (0)1453 542140

Number Eighteen

In lovely Tetbury, with its delis and antique shops, a Tardis-like town house awaits. Four bedrooms are spread over three floors, all have great beds, fluffy robes and beautiful fabrics, and two have bathrooms that would not look out of place in the poshest hotel. The top floor is a great space for a family, with kitchenette, breakfast bar and low beams. Downstairs, the kitchen centres round the Aga; big clocks, art and unique bits of crockery give it a retro feel. Outside is an enclosed garden with a sweet painted fence and an old 'Tabac' sign. Walkers and wanderers: Westonbirt Arboretum and the Cotswold Way are close.

Price	£1,400-£1,795 per week. Short breaks £975.
Rooms	House for 9 (10 with sofabed): 4 doubles, 1 family room.
Meals	Self-catering.
Closed	Rarely
Directions	Given on booking.

Liz Howe
18 Gumstoll Hill, Tetbury GL8 8DG
Tel   +44 (0)1666 504774
Web   www.18gumstoolhill.com

Lodge Farm

A plum Cotswolds position, a striking garden, a rolling programme of improvements, exceptional linen – there are plenty of reasons to stay here. Then there are your flexible hosts, who can help wedding groups, give you supper en famille next to the Aga or something smart and candlelit round the dining-room table: perfect for a house party. The sitting room has flowers, family photographs and lots of magazines; sometimes home-produced lamb for dinner, always excellent coffee at breakfast, homemade bread and their own free-range eggs. Peace and quiet lovers will delight, yet you are a short walk from Tetbury.

Price	£70–£80. Singles from £60. Family suite £95.
Rooms	4: 2 twins/doubles; 1 twin/double, 1 family suite sharing bath.
Meals	Dinner, 2-3 courses, £15–£25. Pub/bistro 2.5 miles.
Closed	Rarely.
Directions	From Cirencester A433 to Tetbury, right B4014 to Avening. After 250 yds, left onto Chavenage Lane. Lodge Farm 1.3 miles on right; left of barn on drive.

Entry 21 Map 1

Robin & Nicky Salmon
Chavenage, Tetbury GL8 8XW
Tel +44 (0)1666 505339
Web www.lodgefarm.co.uk

Sandpipers

On a 500-acre nature reserve in the Cotswold Water Park, criss-crossed by miles of flat foot and cycle path, is a striking lakeside house for ten. The first floor's living area, with its glass main wall, has a bird's-eye view of the lakes: recline on the balcony and absorb the scene. Three clean-cut bedrooms are downstairs, and the cosy master is on the second floor; paintings, books, magazines make you feel at home. The bunk room, at the back, is designed with children in mind. You can use the on-site gym, sauna, spa, steam room, three pools, and can walk to the pub. The honey-stoned loveliness of the Cotswolds is a short drive away.

Price	£1,000–£1,950 per week.
Rooms	House for 10: 3 doubles, 1 twin, 1 bunk room for 2.
Meals	Self-catering.
Closed	5 January to 5 February.
Directions	Given on booking.

Nick & Kate Plummer
21 Clearwater, Lower Mill Estate,
Somerford Keynes, Cirencester GL7 6FJ

Tel   +44 (0)1285 860063
Web   www.cotswoldlakehouses.com

Kempsford Manor

On the edge of the Cotswolds, this 17th-century village manor house is surrounded by large hedges and mature trees. Crunch up the gravelled drive to find floor-to-ceiling windows, dark floors with patterned rugs, wood panelling, a piano and a library. Spacious bedrooms have super garden views; one comes with a Chinese theme, a mix of rugs and blankets and a pretty quilt. Bathrooms are functional and old-fashioned. Beautifully tended gardens (snowdrops are special here) lead to an orchard and a canal walk; stoke up on Zehra's homemade muesli and bread and return for dinner – vegetables are home-grown. *Garden open for NGS.*

Price	£60–£70. Singles £40.
Rooms	3: 2 doubles, 1 single sharing 2 bathrooms.
Meals	Dinner by arrangement. Pub 200 yds.
Closed	Open all year.
Directions	A419 Cirencester-Swindon; Kempsford is signed with Fairford. Right into village, past small village green; on right, through stone columns. Glass front door, by a fountain.

Entry 23 Map 2

Zehra I Williamson
High Street, Kempsford, Fairford GL7 4EQ

Tel   +44 (0)1285 810131
Web   www.kempsfordmanor.com

Lady Lamb Farm

Light pours into perfectly proportioned rooms through windows hung with velvet and chintz; Jeanie and James, farmers, inventors, built the honey-stone house years ago and have kept their Cotswold dream ship-shape. You can play tennis and swim in the pool; bedrooms are a good size and have attractive furniture. Aga breakfasts are scrumptious and served in the striped dining hall with wood-burner, country art and views to the garden: locally cured bacon, fruit and eggs from the chickens that strut on the manicured lawn. Fishing, cycling and golf can be organised for you; Kelmscott Manor, Bibury, Burford and Buscot are close.

Price	From £75. Singles £45.
Rooms	2: 1 twin; 1 twin/double with separate bath.
Meals	Pubs/restaurants 1-4 miles.
Closed	Christmas & New Year.
Directions	Farm 1 mile on right from Meysey Hampton crossroads going towards Fairford on A417.

	Jeanie Keyser
	Meysey Hampton, Cirencester GL7 5LH
Tel	+44 (0)1285 712206
Web	www.ladylambfarm.com

Entry 24 Map 2

The Old Rectory

English to the core – and to the bottom of its lovely garden, with a woodland walk and plenty of quiet places to sit. You sweep into the circular driveway to a yellow labrador welcome. This beautiful 17th-century high gabled house is comfortably lived-in with an understated décor, antiques, creaky floorboards and a real sense of history. The bedrooms, one with a garden view, have very good beds, a chaise longue or an easy chair; bathrooms are vintage but large. Caroline is calm and competent and serves breakfasts with organic eggs and local bacon at the long polished table in the rich red dining room. A special place.

Price	£80–£95. Singles from £50.
Rooms	2: 1 double, 1 twin/double.
Meals	Pub 200 yds.
Closed	December & January.
Directions	South through village from A417. Right after Masons Arms. House 200 yds on left, through stone pillars.

Roger & Caroline Carne
Meysey Hampton, Cirencester GL7 5JX

Tel	+44 (0)1285 851200
Web	www.meyseyoldrectory.co.uk

Ewen Wharf

Life, colour and warmth fill Fiona's pretty early 19th-century wharf keeper's cottage, which snoozes in a tranquil corner of the Cotswolds. A log fire blazes in the cosy low-beamed sitting room, a little Norfolk terrier wags enthusiastically, porcelain marches proudly over shelves and you may recognise art by Fiona's father-in-law – creator of the famous Guinness advertisements. A pleasure to take tea in the well-tended garden, slumber deeply in plump, comfortable beds, chat to Fiona over bacon and eggs from the local farm. Stride out on the Thames Path or stroll to the village pub. Such a peaceful home – and good value too.

Price	£70-£75. Singles £45.
Rooms	2: 1 twin/double, 1 twin sharing bath (let to same party only).
Meals	Pub/restaurant 1 mile.
Closed	Christmas & New Year.
Directions	From Cirencester follow signs to south west and Tetbury. 2 miles, left onto A429 to Kemble. After 1 mile, left to Ewen. House on right before bridge.

Fiona Gilroy
Kemble, Cirencester GL7 6BP

| Tel | +44 (0)1285 770469 |
| Web | www.ewenwharf.co.uk |

The New Inn at Coln

The New Inn is old – 1632 to be exact – but these days, it's all rather smart. It stands in a handsome village with ivy roaming on old stone walls and a sun-trapping terrace. Airy interiors come with low ceilings, painted beams, flagged floors and open fires. There are padded window seats, eastern busts, gilt mirrors and armchairs in the bar, while bedrooms are a treat, all warmly elegant with perfect white linen. Wonky floors and the odd beam in the main house, and bold colours in the old dovecote – along with views across water meadows to the river. Set off for Bibury, Burford, or Stow, then come home to a wonderful meal.

Price	£95–£150. Singles from £85. Half-board from £75 p.p.
Rooms	13 doubles.
Meals	Main courses £5–£35. Sunday lunch £19–£24.
Closed	Rarely.
Directions	From Oxford, A40 past Burford, B4425 for Bibury. Left after Aldsworth to Coln St. Aldwyns.

Stuart Hodges
Main St, Coln St Aldwyns, Cirencester GL7 5AN

Tel   +44 (0)1285 750651
Web   www.new-inn.co.uk

Bathurst Arms

James Walker has worked hard to breathe new life into this handsome inn on the Bathurst Estate. No longer unloved, the 17th-century building exudes warmth and energy as locals, walkers and travellers drop in for pints of Wickwar Cotswold Way – and unpretentious, delicious pub food. Eat here or next door in the revamped restaurant, with open kitchen and a sitting area that displays the wine list – pick a bottle from the shelf. Spruced-up bedrooms, two with white four-posters, provide a homely base for city folk escaping to the Cotswolds: clean, comfortable, freshly painted and TV-free. Ask for a room with a view.

Price	From £75. Singles £55.
Rooms	7 twins/doubles.
Meals	Main courses £9.95-£16.95; bar meals £3.95-£8.95.
Closed	Rarely.
Directions	Beside A435 Cirencester-Cheltenham road, 4 miles north of Cirencester.

James Walker
North Cerney, Cirencester GL7 7BZ

Tel	+44 (0)1285 831281
Web	www.bathurstarms.com

Lower Wiggold Cottage

Peace envelops this bright stone cottage, among fields that the owner's family has farmed for generations. And it has been kitted out with the environment in mind: solar panels, logs from the coppice, water from a bore hole... Indian-style furnishings mingle with reclaimed wood, and there's a lovely sunny yellow kitchen. Pad upstairs to two calm bedrooms; the double bed is carved out of a cherry tree. With an organic farm shop and café on site, your own pretty garden and woodland walks from the door, there's no reason to leave. But, if you do venture out of this bubble, you'll find the whole of the Cotswolds within easy reach.

Price	£495-£600 per week. Short breaks available.
Rooms	Cottage for 4: 1 double, 1 twin.
Meals	Self-catering.
Closed	Rarely.
Directions	Given on booking.

Hilary Chester-Master
Burford Road, Cirencester GL7 5EZ

Tel   +44 (0)1285 640441
Web www.theorganicfarmshop.co.uk

107 Gloucester Street

Slip through gates into a narrow courtyard of potted shrubs and honey-coloured Cotswold stone. This modest Georgian merchant's house is three minutes from the charming town centre yet blissfully quiet. Inside: buttery colours, well-loved antiques, soft uncluttered spaces. Restful, understated bedrooms are small, chic and spotless. Kitchen breakfasts overlook the sheltered garden – a verdant spot for relaxing in summer. For evenings, a creamy first-floor sitting room with a small log fire. Ethne and her ex-army husband are full of fun and good humour – very special.

Price	£75. Singles £50.
Rooms	2: 1 double, 1 twin.
Meals	Hotel 300 yds & restaurants 8-minute walk.
Closed	Christmas & Easter. (Enquire by email only in February.)
Directions	Directions on booking.

Brendan & Ethne McGuinness
Cirencester GL7 2DW

Tel	+44 (0)1285 657861
Web	www.107gloucesterstreet.co.uk

The Ragged Cot

The fine old coaching inn stands alongside 600 acres of National Trust common land. Its several popular bars have exposed stone walls, while the dining room overlooks a large garden. The nine rooms, named after Penguin classics, are cosy and contemporary with king-size beds, walk-in showers and harmonious fabrics. The rest of the pub is just as smart; expect quirky touches, framed pictures of film stars, piles of logs and a stag's head or two. In the kitchen, chefs use local supplies as well as herbs and vegetables from the garden for country dishes served at new pine tables. Wellies, dogs and children are also made welcome.

Price	£95–£120.
Rooms	9 twins/doubles.
Meals	Main courses £10–£15; bar meals from £3.
Closed	Never.
Directions	Follow signs to Minchinhampton off A419 midway between Cirencester and Stroud; pub at x-road east of village.

	Tom Nunn
	Cirencester Road, Chalford, Stroud GL6 8PE
Tel	+44 (0)1453 884643
Web	www.theraggedcot.co.uk

Well Farm

Perhaps it's the gentle, unstuffy attitude of Kate and Edward. Or the great position of the house with its glorious views across the valley. Whichever, you'll feel comforted and invigorated by your stay. It's a real family home and you get both a fresh, pretty bedroom that feels very private and the use of a comfortable, book-filled sitting room opening to a pretty courtyard: Kate is an inspired gardener. Sleep soundly on the softest of pillows, wake to the deep peace of the countryside and the delicious prospect of eggs from their own hens, local sausages and good bacon. The area teems with great walks.

Price	From £80.
Rooms	1 twin/double & sitting room.
Meals	Dinner from £20. Pubs nearby.
Closed	Rarely.
Directions	Directions on booking.

Kate & Edward Gordon Lennox
Frampton Mansell, Stroud GL6 8JB
Tel   +44 (0)1285 760651
Web   www.well-farm.co.uk

Entry 32 Map 1

Nation House

Three cottages were knocked together to create this wisteria-clad, listed village house, now a terrific B&B. Beams are exposed, walls are pale and hung with prints, floors are close-carpeted, the sitting room is formally cosy and quiet. Smart, comfortable bedrooms have patchwork quilts, low beams and padded seats at lattice windows; the bathroom is spotless and the shower room gleaming. In summer, breakfast in the conservatory on still-warm homemade bread, local bacon and sausages, Brenda's preserves. The village is a Cotswold treasure, with two good eating places and with many walks from the door.

Price	£70–£85. Singles £50.
Rooms	3: 1 family; 2 doubles sharing bath (let to same party only).
Meals	Pubs 50 yds.
Closed	Rarely.
Directions	From Cirencester A419 for Stroud. After 7 miles right to Bisley. Left at village shop. House 50 yds on right.

Brenda & Mike Hammond
George Street, Bisley GL6 7BB
Tel   +44 (0)1452 770197

Entry 33 Map 3

Frampton Court

Deep authenticity in this magnificent Grade I-listed house. The manor of Frampton-on-Severn has been in the family since the 11th century and although Rollo and Janie look after the estate, it is Gillian who greets you on behalf of the family and looks after you (very well). Exquisite examples of decorative woodwork and, in the hall, a cheerful log fire; perch on the Mouseman fire seat. Bedrooms are traditional with antiques, panelling and long views. Beds have fine linen, one with embroidered Jacobean hangings. Stroll around the ornamental canal, soak up the old-master views. An architectural masterpiece.

Price	£110–£150.
Rooms	3: 1 twin/double, 1 double, 1 four-poster.
Meals	Dinner £29. Pub across the green. Restaurant 3 miles.
Closed	Rarely.
Directions	M5 junc. 13 west, then B4071. Left down village green, 400 yds, then look to left. 2nd turning left, between two chestnut trees & through ornamental gates in wall.

Rollo & Janie Clifford
Frampton-on-Severn GL2 7EQ

Tel	+44 (0)1452 740267
Web	www.framptoncourtestate.co.uk

The True Heart

A pretty, late-Georgian cottage (and a pub until the 60s), The True Heart is aptly named; heart-warming B&B links arms with sustainability and sincerity. Wake up to a locally sourced full English served in the flower-lined front garden or the cosy bohemian dining room, a friendly mix of modern and antique. There are bathrooms with solar-heated showers, and pure cotton sheets in the south-facing bedrooms. Your vivacious hostess Veronica will share her joyful approach to life and down-to-earth green vision. Leave the petrol-guzzler at home: Frampton, with its immense village green, is too pretty to be clogged with cars.

Price	£85. Singles £55.
Rooms	3: 1 double en suite; 1 double, 1 twin sharing bath.
Meals	Restaurants within walking distance.
Closed	Never.
Directions	From M5 exit 13, A38 for Bristol; 2nd right almost opp. Texaco garage. 1st left thro' village green; entrance 0.6 miles on right, before turn to Vicarage Lane.

Veronica Metcalfe
The Street, Frampton-on-Severn GL2 7ED

Tel	+44 (0)1452 740504
Web	www.thetrueheart.co.uk

St Annes

Step off the narrow pavement into a sunny hall and a welcome to match. Iris worked in tourism for years and lives here with antique restorer Greg, two smiling children and Rollo the dog. They've also made this pretty 17th-century house in the centre of a captivating village (some road noise) as eco-friendly as possible. The biggest and most beautiful bedroom has a four-poster and a bathroom down the hall; the smallish double and the twin rooms will charm you. Farmer's market breakfasts are a warm, stylish feast. As for Painswick, it is known as 'the Queen of the Cotswolds'. *Minimum stay two nights at weekends April-Sept.*

Price	£65. Singles £40.
Rooms	3: 1 double, 1 twin; 1 four-poster with separate bathroom.
Meals	Packed lunch £5. Restaurants/pubs in village.
Closed	Rarely.
Directions	A46 Stroud to Painswick; in Painswick, left after lights; house 3rd door on right. Bus: from Cheltenham & Stroud.

Iris McCormick
Gloucester Street, Painswick GL6 6QN

Tel	+44 (0)1452 812879
Web	www.st-annes-painswick.co.uk

Entry 36 Map 3

The Pinetum Lodge

A year-round Gloucestershire retreat. Come for sheets of snowdrops in January, the nightingale's song in spring, stunning foliage in autumn – and delightful hosts. Their home is a hunting lodge with views over the rolling Cotswold Hills from homely bedrooms with new beds and bathrooms. Enter an enchanted wood surrounded by a RSPB sanctuary and an arboretum planted by Thomas Gambier Parry in 1844 – the scent of pine wafts into the house. Carol and David give you home-grown veg for dinner, there are 13 acres and a fabulous treehouse to explore, and it truly is secluded and peaceful here – rediscover your soul.

Price	£70–£80. Singles £45.
Rooms	3 doubles.
Meals	Dinner £22.50. Pub/restaurant 3 miles.
Closed	Rarely.
Directions	After r'bout with A48, follow A40 (Ross) for 0.7 miles. Right where white line goes double into drive of black & white cottage at speed camera sign on left; track into woods; thro' gates; drive round to front door.

Entry 37 Map 3

David & Carol Wilkin
Churcham GL2 8AD

Tel	+44 (0)1452 750554
Web	www.pinetumlodge.co.uk

5 Ewlyn Road

In a bustling suburb of Cheltenham, Barbara's red-brick villa remains firmly unmodernised. The whiff of beeswax fills the air and Barbara looks after you with old-fashioned ease; the front room has an open fire where you can read a book or chat. Your bedroom is peaceful, the bed is firm, and the white cotton sheets robustly pressed; the clean and purposeful bathroom is shared but not noticeably. In the warm parlour Barbara gives you freshly squeezed orange juice, best Gloucester Old Spot bacon, sausage and free-range eggs – have it outside the sunny back door in summer. Authentic, great value B&B.

Price	£50. Singles £25.
Rooms	1 twin sharing bath (& separate shower).
Meals	Pubs/restaurants 5-minute walk.
Closed	Rarely.
Directions	From A40, signs to Stroud. Up Bath Road past shops; at mini roundabout bear left, then left signed Emmanuel Church. House 2nd on right; front door to side.

Barbara Jameson
Cheltenham GL53 7PB

Tel   +44 (0)1242 261243

The Maisonette

In Cheltenham's elegant centre, a second-floor apartment in a Regency townhouse overlooking Montpellier Gardens. Be met by fresh flowers, soft sofas and light flooding in from sash windows. There's a gleaming kitchen, an antique dining table, and the splendid gardens. The sheer luxury is a delight: spotless bathrooms, scrumptious breakfast hampers on request; there are cots and highchairs if you need them and fun fabrics and warm colours brighten cosy bedrooms. It's as peaceful as can be. Posh but friendly, and the service comes with a big smile. *Three apartments for two in the same building also available.*

Price	£980 per week.
Rooms	Apartment for 4: 2 twins/doubles.
Meals	Self-catering.
Closed	Never.
Directions	Given on booking.

Sophie Thompson
16 Montpellier Spa Road, Cheltenham GL50 1UL

Tel	+44 (0)1780 460407
Web	www.cheltenhamapartments.co.uk

Hanover House

The former home of Elgar's wife, set in an early-Victorian terrace in Cheltenham's heart, is warm, elegant, inviting – and surprisingly peaceful. There are big trees all around and the river Chelt laps at the foot of the garden. Inside, a graceful period décor is enlivened by Bracken and Sophie (the dogs!) and exuberant splashes of colour; the delectable drawing room, with pale walls and trio of arched windows, is the perfect foil for paintings, books and rugs. Bedrooms have vivid Indian throws, bathrooms are simple and stylish. But best of all are Veronica and James: musical, well-travelled, irresistible.

Price	£80–£100. Singles £60–£70.
Rooms	3: 1 double; 1 double, 1 twin each with separate bath.
Meals	Pubs/restaurants 500 yds.
Closed	Rarely.
Directions	In Cheltenham town centre, 200 yds from bus/coach station; 600 yds from railway station. Parking available.

Veronica & James Ritchie
65 St George's Road, Cheltenham GL50 3DU
Tel   +44 (0)1242 541297
Web   www.hanoverhouse.org

Entry 40 Map 3

The Courtyard Studio

This new first-floor studio, attractive in reclaimed red brick, is reached via its own wrought-iron staircase; you are beautifully private. The friendly owners live next door, and will cook you a delicious breakfast in the house, or leave you a continental one in your own fridge. Find a clever, compact, contemporary space with a light and uncluttered living area, a mini window seat opposite two very comfortable boutique hotel style beds, fine linen, wicker armchair, and a patio area for balmy days. A 20-minute walk will take you to the centre of Cheltenham and you're a two-minute canter from the races. *Minimum stay two nights.*

Price	£75.
Rooms	1 twin.
Meals	Restaurants/pubs within 1 mile.
Closed	Rarely.
Directions	From racecourse roundabout on A435 towards town centre, turn right on to Cleevelands Drive (telephone and old postbox), 300 metres on left, drive through brick portal gateway. No 1 is in left corner.

John & Annette Gill
1 The Cleevelands Courtyard,
Cleevelands Drive, Cheltenham GL50 4QF

Entry 41 Map 3   Tel   +44 (0)1242 573125

Green Dragon

Hidden down a sleepy lane somewhere off the A435, this mellow Cotswold stone building, festooned with honeysuckle, was a cider house three centuries ago. It's still beautifully traditional inside. Settle down with a pint of Hooky in the stone-flagged bar, all warm mustard walls and glowing candles, logs in the inglenook, hops hanging from the beams. The food is lovely and the pick of the courtyard-annexe bedrooms is the St George's Suite, a vast room above the former stables, with leather sofas, a king-size bed and huge bathroom with free standing bath and walk-in shower. Wonderful walks start from the front door.

Price	£85–£140. Singles £65.
Rooms	9: 8 twins/doubles, 1 suite.
Meals	Main courses £7.50–£15.95.
Closed	Rarely.
Directions	Cockleford is signed off A435 at Elkstone south of Cheltenham.

Simon & Nicky Haly
Cockleford, Cowley, Cheltenham GL53 9NW

Tel	+44 (0)1242 870271
Web	www.green-dragon-inn.co.uk

Entry 42 Map 3

Beaumont House

This is just what you'd want of a small B&B hotel: stylish bedrooms, excellent breakfasts, value for money, owners who care. Fan and Alan have lived all over the world and came back to set up a hotel they'd like to stay in themselves. Inside, there's a beautiful sitting room with huge windows and a tempting honesty bar. Spotless bedrooms cover three floors. Some are simpler with attractive prices, others are nothing short of extravagant, but all come with good bathrooms, so every budget will be happy here. Breakfast is served in an elegant dining room (high ceilings, garden views), while Cheltenham is a 15-minute stroll.

Price	£84–£170. Singles from £65.
Rooms	16: 10 doubles, 3 twins/doubles, 1 family room, 2 singles.
Meals	Restaurants within walking distance; room service available Monday-Thursday evenings.
Closed	Rarely.
Directions	Leave one-way system in centre of town for Stroud (south) on A46. Straight ahead, through lights and right at 1st mini-roundabout. On left after 500m.

Alan & Fan Bishop
56 Shurdington Road, Cheltenham GL53 0JE

Tel	+44 (0)1242 223311
Web	www.bhhotel.co.uk

Inn at Fossebridge

A vast two-acre lake, hog roasts in summer, a glorious old bar – such details set the old coaching inn apart. Inside all is super-rustic and cosy – flagstone floors, stone walls, open fires, beamed ceilings – with a terrific hubbub at lunchtime. The Jenkins family run this old coaching inn and draw in lovers of good food with blackboard specials. The bar is divided by stone archways; the dining room has a gentler Georgian feel, and there's a sitting room in country-house style. Outside: a four-acre garden bordering the river Coln. Country-smart bedrooms are decorated in Georgian style and range from smallish to spacious.

Price	£120–£160. Singles £110–£145.
Rooms	8: 7 twins/doubles, 1 family suite.
Meals	Main courses £10.95–£16.95; bar meals £5.95–£8.50; Sunday roast £12.95.
Closed	Rarely.
Directions	Beside A429 between Cirencester & Northleach.

Robert & Samantha Jenkins
Fossebridge, Cheltenham GL54 3JS
Tel   +44 (0)1285 720721
Web   www.fossebridgeinn.co.uk

Entry 44 Map 3

The Wheatsheaf Inn

This former wool market town is tucked between pretty hills on the Roman Fosse Way. Big smiles from a young staff greet you and a pint of Hooky Bitter will be in your hand before you know it. The worn flagstones in the well-stocked bar separate two dining areas aglow with wooden floors, striking Asian rugs and crackling fires. Expect a mix of traditional English fare of unpretentious goodness and impeccable provenance. Bedrooms are calm and spacious, many with wooden headboards and period fabrics. A brilliant little place to return to after a day out exploring the High Wold countryside, with a youthful buzz.

Price	£80–£100.
Rooms	9 twins/doubles.
Meals	Main courses £10–£17; set menus £12 & £15.
Closed	Open all day.
Directions	In village centre, off A429 between Stow & Burford.

	Sam & Georgina Pearman
	West End, Northleach, Cheltenham GL54 3EZ
Tel	+44 (0)1451 860244
Web	www.cotswoldswheatsheaf.com

Entry 45 Map 3

Sherborne Forge

You are in a quiet corner of the Cotswolds, in your own restored cottage across the courtyard from the owner's 17th-century house and overlooking Sherborne Brook. Walk in to a large living space with a high beamed ceiling, comfy sofas, bright rugs, antiques, flowers, books and a dining table and chairs. You have your own small kitchen for toast and tea; Karen brings over a delicious organic breakfast, served on a private terrace on sunny mornings. Your bedroom has pretty fabrics and fine linen; the bathroom has a big tub for long soaks. Fish for trout in the brook, head off for glorious walks and bike rides; this is a sanctuary.

Price	From £90. Singles £70.
Rooms	1 double with sitting room.
Meals	Pub/restaurant 3 miles.
Closed	Never.
Directions	A429 at Northleach; A40 towards Oxford. 3 miles, left signed Clapton & Sherborne. After 1 mile, left signed Farmington & Turkdean. 400 yds past houses, right before 30mph exit sign. 100 yds down small lane to house.

Karen Kelly
Number 1 Sherborne, Cheltenham GL54 3DW

Tel	+44 (0)1451 844286
Web	www.sherborneforge.co.uk

Clapton Manor

Karin and James's 16th-century manor is as all homes should be: loved and lived-in. And, with three-foot-thick walls, flagstoned floors, sit-in fireplaces and stone-mullioned windows, it's gorgeous. The enclosed garden, full of birdsong and roses, wraps itself around the house. One bedroom has a secret door that leads to a fuchsia-pink bathroom; the other room, smaller, is wallpapered in a honeysuckle trellis and has wonderful garden views. Wellies, dogs, barbours, log fires… and breakfast by a vast Tudor fireplace on homemade bread and jams and eggs from the hens. A happy, charming family home.

Price	From £95. Singles £85.
Rooms	2: 1 double, 1 twin/double.
Meals	Pub/restaurants within 15-minute drive.
Closed	Rarely.
Directions	A429 Cirencester-Stow. Right signed Sherborne & Clapton. In village, pass grassy area to left, postbox in one corner; house straight ahead on left on corner, facing down hill.

Karin & James Bolton
Clapton-on-the-Hill, Cheltenham GL54 2LG

Tel	+44 (0)1451 810202
Web	www.claptonmanor.co.uk

The Dial House Hotel

Bourton – Venice of the Cotswolds – is bisected by the Windrush; willow branches bathe in its waters. Dial House is equally alluring, so skip past the trim lawns and find the old world made new. Mullioned windows and stone fireplaces shine warmly, armchairs are dressed in Zoffany, Cole & Son wallpaper sparkles on some walls. Escape the hordes and take lunch in the garden at the back. Fabulous food in the restaurant, cool colours in the bar, and bedrooms in different shapes and sizes, from grand four-posters in the main house to airy pastels and silky quilts in the coach house annexe. *Minimum stay two nights at weekends.*

Price	£120–£220.
Rooms	13: 10 doubles, 2 four-posters, 1 suite.
Meals	Lunch from £4.95. Dinner, 3 courses, about £40.
Closed	Never.
Directions	From Oxford, A40 to Northleach, right on A429 to Bourton. Hotel set back from High St opposite main bridge.

Martyn & Elaine Booth
Bourton-on-the-Water, Cheltenham GL54 2AN

Tel +44 (0)1451 822244
Web www.dialhousehotel.com

Lords of the Manor

The setting is spectacular, eight acres of lush lawns and formal gardens flanked by the river Eye. Step in to find parquet flooring, mullioned windows, roaring fires and porters' chairs in a sitting-room bar. Fabrics come courtesy of Osborne & Little, views from the drawing room spin down to the river, old oils adorn the walls. There's a complimentary wine tasting for guests on Saturday evenings, not a bad way to choose your tipple before sitting down to a Michelin-starred dinner... Smart bedrooms come in contemporary country-house style with excellent art, padded bedheads, bowls of fruit. Church bells chime on Sunday.

Price	£191–£303. Suites £362–£380. Half-board from £130.50 p.p.
Rooms	26: 21 twins/doubles, 5 suites.
Meals	Lunch from £19.50. Dinner, 4 courses, £55. Tasting menu £65.
Closed	Never.
Directions	North from Cirencester on A429 for 17 miles; left for The Slaughters. In Lower Slaughter, left over bridge, into Upper Slaughter. On right in village, signed.

Ingo Wiangke
Upper Slaughter, Cheltenham GL54 2JD

Tel	+44 (0)1451 820243
Web	www.lordsofthemanor.com

Rectory Farmhouse

Once a monastery, now a farmhouse with style. Passing a development of converted farm buildings to reach the Rectory's warm Cotswold stones makes the discovery doubly exciting. More glory within: Sybil, a talented designer, has created something immaculate, fresh and uplifting. A wood-burner glows in the sitting room, bed linen is white, walls cream; beds are superb, bathrooms sport cast-iron slipper baths and power showers and views are to the church. Sybil used to own a restaurant and her breakfasts — by the Aga or in the conservatory under a rampant vine — are a further treat.

Price	From £90. Singles £60.
Rooms	2 doubles.
Meals	Pubs/restaurants 1 mile.
Closed	Christmas & New Year.
Directions	B4068 from Stow to Lower Swell, left just before Golden Ball Inn. Far end of gravel drive on right.

Sybil Gisby
Lower Swell, Cheltenham GL54 1LH
Tel   +44 (0)1451 832351

White Hart Inn

Stow's famous market square goes all the way back to 1107, built on the orders of Henry I. The White Hart appeared a few years later. The bar comes in period colours with stripped floorboards and an open fire, while rustic chic pours through the dining room; here you may dig into Paul's delicious food. Bedrooms upstairs come in different shapes and sizes. The small ones are perfect for a night or two, but if you're staying longer go for the big room overlooking the square. One has a 13th-century window, all share the same country style: low ceilings, wonky floors, papered walls. *Minimum stay two nights at weekends.*

Price	£100–£120. Singles from £75.
Rooms	5: 4 doubles, 1 single.
Meals	Lunch from £5. Dinner, 3 courses, about £25.
Closed	Occasionally.
Directions	M4 junc. 15, A419 north, then A429 for Stow. On the square in town.

Marion & Ken Sibley
The Square, Stow-on-the-Wold,
Cheltenham GL54 1AF

Tel   +44 (0)1451 830674
                         Web   www.whitehartstow.com

Westward

Susie and Jim are highly organised and efficient, juggling farm, horses and B&B. She's also a great cook (Leith trained). The grand, but cosy, house sits above Sudeley Castle surrounded by its own 600 acres; all bedrooms look west to long views. Colours, fabrics and furniture are in perfect harmony, beds and linen are inviting, and the easy mix of elegant living and family bustle is delightful. There's tea on the terrace in summer and by a log fire in winter… your hosts delight in sharing this very English home. Wonderful walks, Cheltenham, Cotswold villages, fabulous restaurants and pubs are near.

Price	From £90. Singles from £60.
Rooms	3: 1 double, 2 twins/doubles.
Meals	Pubs/restaurants 1 mile.
Closed	December & January.
Directions	From Abbey Sq., Winchcombe, go north; after 50 yds, right into Castle St. Follow for 1 mile; after farm buildings, right for Sudeley Lodge; follow for 600 yds. House on right; first oak door.

Susie & Jim Wilson
Sudeley Lodge, Winchcombe,
Cheltenham GL54 5JB

Tel   +44 (0)1242 604372
Web   www.westward-sudeley.co.uk

Wesley House Restaurant

A 15th-century house on Winchcombe's ancient high street; John Wesley stayed in 1755, hence the name. Come for sofas in front of a roaring fire, candles flickering on smartly dressed tables and a fine conservatory for delicious breakfasts. Next door is a newer restaurant, unashamedly contemporary with a smoked-glass bar and alcoves to hide away in. Quirky cosy bedrooms are up in the eaves with a warm country style with good beds, pretty fabrics, small showers, smart carpets and wonky floors. Back downstairs, dig into food as simple or rich as you want, anything from fish cakes or a good burger to a three-course feast.

Price	£80–£95. Singles from £65. Half-board (for 1-night stays on Saturdays) £90–£100 p.p.
Rooms	5: 1 twin, 1 twin/double, 3 doubles.
Meals	Bar & grill: lunch & dinner from £6.50. Restaurant: dinner £19.50–£38. Not Sunday nights.
Closed	Never.
Directions	From Cheltenham, B4632 to Winchcombe. Restaurant on right. Drop off luggage, parking nearby.

Matthew Brown
High Street, Winchcombe, Cheltenham GL54 5LJ

Tel	+44 (0)1242 602366
Web	www.wesleyhouse.co.uk

Wren House

Barely two miles from Stow-on-the-Wold, the peaceful house sits charmingly in a tiny hamlet. The stylish stone house was built before the English Civil War and Kiloran spent two years renovating it; the results are a joy. Downstairs, light-filled, elegant rooms with glowing rugs on pale Cotswold stone; upstairs, delicious bedrooms, spotless bathrooms and a doorway to duck. Breakfast can include cream from the Jerseys over the wall, and the well-planted garden, in which you are encouraged to sit, has far-reaching views. Explore rolling valleys and glorious gardens; Kiloran can advise. *Children over six welcome.*

Price	£90–£100. Singles from £70.
Rooms	2: 1 twin/double; 1 twin/double with separate bath/shower.
Meals	Pubs/restaurants 2 miles.
Closed	Rarely.
Directions	A429 between Stow & Moreton; turn to Donnington; 400 yds, bear left uphill; 100 yds, sign on right in wall beside The Granary Cottage with parking at rear through 5-bar gate.

Kiloran McGrigor
Donnington, Moreton-in-Marsh GL56 0XZ

Tel	+44 (0)1451 831787
Web	www.wrenhouse.net

Entry 54 Map 4

The Old School

Comfortable, warm and filled with understated style is this 1854 Cotswold stone house. Wendy and John are generous, beds are enormous, linen is laundered, towels and robes are thick and fluffy. Your own mini fridge is carefully hidden and lighting is well thought-out. Best of all is the upstairs sitting room: a chic, open-plan space with church style windows letting the light flood in and super sofas, good art, lovely fabrics. A wood-burner keeps you toasty, Wendy is a grand cook and all is flexible. A gorgeous, relaxing place to stay – on the A44 but peaceful at night – where absolutely nothing is too much trouble.

Price	£90. Singles £60.
Rooms	4: 3 doubles, 1 twin/double.
Meals	Dinner, 4 courses, £32. Supper, 2 courses, £18. Supper tray £12. Pub 0.5 miles.
Closed	Rarely.
Directions	From Moreton, A44 for Chipping Norton & Oxford. Little Compton 3.5 miles; stay on main road, then right for Chastleton village. House on corner, immed. left into drive.

Wendy Veale & John Scott-Lee
Little Compton, Moreton-in-Marsh GL56 0SL

Tel	+44 (0)1608 674588
Web	www.theoldschoolbedandbreakfast.com

Entry 55 Map 4

Horse & Groom

This place delivers in spades: a friendly welcome, stylish interiors, terrific food. The inn stands at the top of the hill with views to the side that pour over the Cotswolds. Inside, cool colours, stripped floors, open fires and the odd stone wall for a modern rustic feel. In summer you can sit under the damson trees and watch chefs gather eggs from the coop or carrots from the kitchen garden. Uncluttered bedrooms are plush and come in contemporary country-house style; those at the front are soundproofed against the road. Will cooks, Tom pours the ales, and a cheery conviviality flows. *Minimum stay two nights at weekends.*

Price	£105–£150. Singles from £70. Half-board from £70 p.p.
Rooms	5 doubles.
Meals	Bar meals all day from £9.50. Dinner, à la carte, £25–£35. Not Sunday night.
Closed	Christmas Day & New Year's Eve.
Directions	West from Moreton-in-Marsh on A44. Climb hill in Bourton-on-the-Hill; pub at top on left.

Tom & Will Greenstock
Bourton-on-the-Hill, Moreton-in-Marsh GL56 9AQ

Tel	+44 (0)1386 700413
Web	www.horseandgroom.info

Lower Brook House

The village is a jewel, saved from tourist hordes by roads too narrow for coaches. The house is no less alluring, built in 1624 for workers from the silk mills that made Blockley rich. Find the past on display: flagged floors, mullioned windows, timber-framed walls and heaps of vintage luggage. Logs smoulder in an inglenook in winter; excellent bedrooms (one is small) come in crisp country-house style with beautiful fabrics and pristine linen. Outside, roses climb on walls and a small lawn runs down to a terrace for afternoon tea – as beautifully executed as Anna's breakfasts and dinners. *Minimum stay two nights at weekends.*

Price	£80–£175.
Rooms	6: 3 doubles, 2 twins, 1 four-poster.
Meals	Dinner, 3 courses, £25–£30.
Closed	Christmas.
Directions	A44 west from Moreton-in-Marsh. At top of hill in Bourton-on-the-Hill, right signed Blockley. Down hill to village, on right.

Jullan & Anna Ebbutt
Lower Street, Blockley, Moreton-in-Marsh
GL56 9DS

Tel	+44 (0)1386 700286
Web	www.lowerbrookhouse.com

Skylark Cottage

Hikers, birdwatchers and peace-seekers will love this – a terraced stone cottage on the edge of sweet Blockley, surrounded by woodland and fields; bring your boots and tramp the trails. Oak beams, exposed stone walls and limestone-flagged floors will please you, while the bedrooms are peaceful and cosy, the twin with Victorian-style, metal-frame beds. In your neat Shaker-style kitchen, a tea tray, cake and flowers welcome you on arrival. Then it's down a steep staircase – with stair gate at the top – to the living room, whose large ceiling-to-floor window bathes the space in light and gives glorious views out to the hills.

Price	£300-£600 per week. Short breaks available.
Rooms	Cottage for 4: 1 double; 1 twin.
Meals	Self-catering.
Closed	Never.
Directions	Given on booking.

Ruth Lucas
47 Park Road, Blockley,
Moreton-in-Marsh GL56 9BZ

Tel   +44 (0)1451 832575
Web   www.skylarkcottage.co.uk

The Malt House

In a pretty village of sculpted golden stone sits the Malt House, delightful inside and out. An impeccable garden runs down to a stream; pull up a seat and snooze in the sun. Equally impressive is Judi's kitchen garden which provides flowers for beautiful bedrooms and summer fruits for breakfast. Inside: parquet flooring, sparkling wallpaper, mullioned windows, books and papers, an honesty bar and sofas by the fire. Spotless bedrooms are warmly elegant and hugely comfortable. All this and maps for walkers, lists of restaurants, hot water bottles and umbrellas to keep you dry. *Minimum stay two nights at weekends April-Oct.*

Price	£120–£140. Singles from £85. Suite from £150.
Rooms	7: 1 double, 4 twins/doubles, 1 four-poster, 1 suite.
Meals	Pub 200 yards. Dinner by arrangement (min. 12 people).
Closed	One week over Christmas.
Directions	From Oxford, A44 through Moreton-in-Marsh; right on B4081 north to Chipping Campden. Entering village, 1st right for Broad Campden. Hotel 1 mile on left.

Judi Wilkes
Broad Campden, Chipping Campden GL55 6UU

Tel   +44 (0)1386 840295
Web   www.malt-house.co.uk

Charingworth Manor

This grand old manor house stands in blissful country with views from its garden that shoot south for three miles. Inside, ancient beams and a roaring fire, painted panelling, mullioned windows, and a low-ceilinged restaurant aglow with flickering candles. Bedrooms come in the same soothing style: neutral colours, padded headboards, excellent linen. Some open onto private terraces, others have the odd beam, all have white robes in excellent bathrooms. And there's heaps to do: tennis, croquet, a small gym, an indoor pool, a steam room and sauna… sun loungers too. Parasols shade the terrace, perfect for cream teas.

Price	£125–£240. Suites £195–£295. Singles from £90. Half-board from £97.50 p.p.
Rooms	26: 20 twins/doubles, 6 suites.
Meals	Lunch from £5.25. Sunday lunch from £14.95. Dinner, 3 courses, about £35.
Closed	Never.
Directions	West out of Chipping Campden on B4035 and house signed right after three miles.

Michael Eastick
Charingworth, Chipping Campden GL55 6NS
Tel   +44 (0)1386 593555
Web   www.classiclodges.co.uk

Ebrington Arms

The glorious gardens at Hidcote Manor and Kiftsgate Court are a ramble across fields from the Ebrington Arms. Little has changed in the 17th-century bar, cosy with low beams and winter fires. Bag a seat and share pints of Purity with the regulars, or seek out the delightful stone-flagged dining room next door. Dishes are simple yet full of flavour – and there's no need to negotiate the route home when you can bed down here. Bedrooms, up steepish stairs, are quirky and full of charm: chunky wooden beds, colourful throws, deep window seats with village views. An award-winning pub, and run by the nicest people.

Price	£90–£120.
Rooms	3: 1 twin, 1 double, 1 four-poster.
Meals	Main courses £9.50–£14.50.
Closed	Rarely.
Directions	West from Shipton-on-Stour on B4035. Across A429. After a mile, bear right at sharp left-hand bend; village signed.

Claire & Jim Alexander
Ebrington, Chipping Campden GL55 6NH

Tel	+44 (0)1386 593223
Web	www.theebringtonarms.co.uk

The Kings Hotel

A gorgeous small hotel on the market place of this idyllic town. Flower baskets full of colour hang from stone walls while interiors sparkle in cool rustic style. Find stripped floors in the bar and beams in a super restaurant, where a huge curved settle dominates the room. There's a wood-burner for winter and doors that open onto a terrace and lawn – perfect for summer. Bedrooms are upstairs. Those at the front overlook the square, at the back they have the peace of the garden. All come with pretty beds, crisp linen and lovely bathrooms. The gorgeous countryside demands your walking boots. *Minimum stay two nights at weekends.*

Price	£100–£195. Singles from £88. Half-board from £75 p.p.
Rooms	14: 11 doubles, 3 twins.
Meals	Lunch £12.50–£15.50. Sunday lunch from £9.95. Dinner, £15–£30.
Closed	Never.
Directions	From Oxford, A44 north for Evesham. 5 miles after Moreton-in-Marsh, right on B4081 to Chipping Campden. Hotel in square by town hall.

Charlotte Rides
High Street, Chipping Campden GL55 6AW

Tel	+44 (0)1386 840256
Web	www.kingscampden.co.uk

Corse Lawn House Hotel

Old-fashioned values win out at Corse Lawn. It may not be the fanciest place in the book, but excellent service and generous prices make it a must for those in search of an alternative to contemporary minimalism. This impeccable Queen Anne manor house is also the hub of a small community. In summer you can sit out under parasols and dig into a cream tea while ducks glide by. Inside, slightly eccentric furnishings prevail: palms in the swimming pool, a sofa'd bistro for light meals, a real fire; bedrooms are big, chintzy and hugely comfortable. As for the food, it's all homemade, utterly delicious, and breakfast is a treat.

Price	£150–£170. Suites £185. Singles £95. Half-board from £100 p.p.
Rooms	19: 14 twins/doubles, 2 four-posters, 2 suites, 1 single.
Meals	Lunch & dinner £10–£35.
Closed	Christmas Day & Boxing Day.
Directions	West from Tewkesbury on A438 for Ledbury. After 3 miles left onto B4211. Hotel on right after 2 miles.

Baba Hine
Corse Lawn, Gloucester GL19 4LZ
Tel   +44 (0)1452 780771
Web   www.corselawn.com

Astalleigh House

The views from here to the Malvern Hills are worth the journey alone, but you also get bright, softly-coloured bedrooms with outrageously snuggly beds, the floatiest goose down, and compact bathrooms with generous towels and Body Shop goodies. There's a sitting room with pale walls, lots of books and magazines, jazzy striped cushions on a comfy sofa and interesting paintings of Northumberland – you can flop here happily. Affable Harriet gives you eggs from their hens and delicious sausages and bacon from the local butcher to set you up for grand walks; this is a good romantic escape for those with outdoor tastes.

Price	From £75. Singles £50. (Child £15.)
Rooms	2: 1 double, 1 family.
Meals	Pub/restaurant 0.5 miles.
Closed	Christmas & New Year.
Directions	M5, junction 8, M50 junction 1 north A38. Then 2nd left Ripple, Uckinghall, Equine Hospital, left at crossroads. House first on left. Train to Cheltenham, Gloucester or Pershore.

Harriet & Keith Jewers
School Lane, Ripple, Tewkesbury GL20 6EU
Tel   +44 (0)1684 593740
Web   www.astalleighhouse.co.uk

Upper Court

A splendid Georgian manor in acres of landscaped grounds – all you'd want from a country house. Bring friends for a party, get married, or come for a weekend of romance – you are looked after by family, or lovely staff. Antique furniture, floral flourishes, sumptuous four-poster beds, swish new bathrooms, consummate hosts – and there's heaps to do: tennis, croquet, billiards, an outdoor pool, hill-walking, riding, clay-pigeon shooting. Groups can book dinner, there are art and pottery classes in the stables and a good pub in the village. *Min. two nights at weekends, unless late booking. Self-catering for large parties.*

Price	£95–£120. Singles £75.
Rooms	3: 2 doubles, 1 twin.
Meals	Dinner, for parties only, £35. Pubs/restaurants 3-minute walk.
Closed	Christmas.
Directions	M5 junc. 9, A46 to Teddington Hands; left, follow signs for Kemerton. Left at War Memorial. House directly behind parish church.

Bill & Diana Herford
Kemerton, Tewkesbury GL20 7HY

Tel +44 (0)1386 725351
Web www.uppercourt.co.uk

The Trout at Tadpole Bridge

A very old inn on the banks of the Thames – pick up a pint and watch life float by. The walls are busy with fishing rods, children are liked and dogs can doze in the flagstoned bars. The downstairs is open plan and timber-framed, there are gilt mirrors and logs piled high in alcoves. Bedrooms at the back are away from the crowd, three opening onto a small courtyard, all have funky fabrics, trim carpets, a library of films. Sleigh beds, upholstered armchairs… one even has a roof terrace. Food is as local as possible and there are maps for walkers to keep you thin! *Minimum stay two nights at weekends May-Oct.*

Price	£110. Suite £140. Singles from £75.
Rooms	6: 2 doubles, 3 twins/doubles, 1 suite.
Meals	Main courses £5-£30.
Closed	Rarely.
Directions	A420 southwest from Oxford for Swindon. After 13 miles, right for Tadpole Bridge. Pub on right by bridge.

Gareth & Helen Pugh
Buckland Marsh, Faringdon SN7 8RF

Tel	+44 (0)1367 870382
Web	www.trout-inn.co.uk

Rectory Farm

Come for the happy buzz of family life. It's relaxed and informal and you are welcomed with tea and homemade shortbread by Mary Anne. The date above the entrance stone reads 1629 and bedrooms, light and spotless, have beautiful stone-arched and mullioned windows. The huge twin has ornate plasterwork and views over the garden and church; the double is cosier with a carved pine headboard; both have good showers and large fluffy towels. The pedigree North Devon cattle are Robert's pride and joy and his family has farmed here for three generations. It's a treat to stay. *Minimum stay two nights at weekends & high season.*

Price	£75–£80. Singles £55.
Rooms	2: 1 double, 1 twin.
Meals	Pub 2-minute walk.
Closed	Mid-December to mid-January.
Directions	From Oxford, A420 for Swindon for 8 miles & right at r'bout, for Witney (A415). Over 2 bridges, immed. right by pub car park. Right at T-junc.; drive on right, past church.

Mary Anne Florey
Northmoor, Witney OX29 5SX
Tel   +44 (0)1865 300207
Web   www.oxtowns.co.uk/rectoryfarm

The Fleece

If you need to be in Oxford, staying at the Fleece is an attractive alternative; a cheaper one, too. Lee Cash and Victoria Moon dug deep to buy the lease on the Georgian Fleece – and thus launched the successful Peach Pub Company. Expect an inviting gastropub interior: wooden floors, plum walls, squashy sofas, low tables – and continental opening hours that start with coffee and bacon sarnies at 8.30am. Thumbs-up too for the all-day sandwiches, salads and deli-board menu. Delightful bedrooms are big enough to hold an armchair or two and beds are very comfortable; we'd recommend one at the front overlooking Witney's green.

Price	£80–£100.
Rooms	10: 8 doubles, 1 twin, 1 family room.
Meals	Main courses £9.75–£19.50; bar meals £4–£12.
Closed	Christmas Day.
Directions	Witney is off A40 between Oxford and Burford; pub on green, near church.

Aimee Moore
11 Church Green, Witney OX28 4AZ

Tel   +44 (0)1993 892270
Web   www.fleecewitney.co.uk

The Bird in Hand

Super food, good prices and understated country style are the hallmarks of this welcoming inn. Come for crackling fires, varnished floorboards and exposed stone walls. Large bedrooms are found behind, in converted outbuildings that open onto a lawned courtyard. Expect big pine beds, adequate bathrooms and crisp white linen. Back in the restaurant delicious homemade food draws a crowd; Sundays are occasionally busy with classic car clubs dropping by for lunch, bringing unexpected glamour to the vast car park. Woodstock, Stow and Burford are all close and the excellent Cornbury music festival takes place up the road in July.

Price	£80–£110. Family room £90–£130. Singles from £70.
Rooms	15: 11 doubles, 2 twins, 2 family rooms.
Meals	Lunch & dinner £5–£25.
Closed	Rarely.
Directions	On B4022 Witney-Charlbury road, 3 miles north of Witney.

Barry Shelton
Whiteoak Green, Hailey, Witney OX29 9XP

Tel   +44 (0)1993 868321
Web   www.birdinhandinn.co.uk

Old Bank Hotel

Stroll south past Corpus Christi to Christ Church meadows, head north for All Souls. Back at the Old Bank, warm contemporary elegance comes with an important collection of modern art and photography which adorns all walls including those of the bedrooms. There's a lively bar/brasserie with fine arched windows for cocktails and meals, and bedrooms are exemplary, the biggest with sofas. Service is serene, curtains are pleated, beds are turned down, the papers are delivered to your door. Breakfast is served in the courtyard in summer, off-street parking is priceless, and walking tours led by an art historian are free for guests.

Price	£135–£325. Singles from £160.
Rooms	42: 29 doubles, 12 twins/doubles, 1 suite for 2-5.
Meals	Breakfast £11.95–£12.95. Lunch & dinner £10–£30.
Closed	Never.
Directions	Cross Magdalen Bridge for city centre. Straight through 1st set of lights, then left into Merton St. Follow road right; 1st right into Magpie Lane. Car park 2nd right.

Ben Truesdale
92-94 High Street, Oxford OX1 4BN
Tel   +44 (0)1865 799599
Web   www.oldbank-hotel.co.uk

Old Parsonage Hotel

A country house in the city, with a friendly bar for a drop of champagne, a rooftop terrace for afternoon tea and a hidden garden where you can listen to the bells of St Giles. Logs smoulder in the original stone fireplace, the daily papers wait by an ancient window and exquisite art hangs on the walls. You feast in the restaurant on meat from the owner's Oxfordshire farm, then retire to warm stylish bedrooms which are scattered all over the place – some at the front, others in a sympathetic extension. Historical walking tours are 'on the house', while the hotel owns a punt on the Cherwell and will pack you a picnic. Brilliant.

Price	£150–£225. Suites £250.
Rooms	31: 22 twins/doubles, 7 suites for 3, 1 for 4.
Meals	Breakfast £12–£14. Lunch & dinner £10–£45.
Closed	Never.
Directions	From A40 ring road, south onto Banbury Road thro' Summertown. Hotel on right just before St Giles Church.

Deniz Dustanel
1 Banbury Road, Oxford OX2 6NN

Tel   +44 (0)1865 310210
Web   www.oldparsonage-hotel.co.uk

71 Charlbury Road

An excellent Oxford address, frequent buses or a 25-minute walk to town, traditionally comfortable, utterly peaceful. Jacqueline, talented needlewoman, pianist and ex-stewardess, pays gentle attention to housekeeping and guests, yet never intrudes. Up carpeted stairs are comfy-cosy bedrooms with Vi-Spring mattresses and, in the double, a hand-made patchwork quilt. Spotless bathrooms are stocked with towels and bedroom windows face the garden; college playing fields stretch beyond. The sitting room has pale sofas, velvet armchairs, a harpsichord, a grand piano – let Jacqueline treat you to a little Chopin!

Price	£70. Singles £45.
Rooms	2: 1 single; 1 double with separate bathroom.
Meals	Pubs/restaurants 0.5 miles.
Closed	Christmas, New Year & February.
Directions	North out of Oxford on A4165, Banbury Road, take 6th exit on right, Belbroughton Road. Left at the end into Charlbury Road; 2nd turning on right, first house on left.

Mrs Jacqueline Burgess
Oxford OX2 6UX

Tel   +44 (0)1865 511752

Manor Farmhouse

Helen and John radiate pleasure and good humour in this old Cotswold stone farmhouse, once part of the Blenheim estate (a short walk down the lane). Find comfortable, traditional living with good prints and paintings, venerable furniture and nothing cluttered or overdone. Shallow, curvy, 18th-century stairs lead up to the pretty double; the small bedroom has a challenging spiral stair to a cobbled courtyard. Breakfast is by the stone fireplace and ancient dresser. On warm days have tea in a sheltered corner by the fig tree and pots, and wander in the lovely garden; the village is quiet yet close to Oxford.

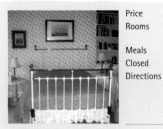

Price	£70–£78. Singles from £60.
Rooms	2 doubles, sharing shower room (let to same party only).
Meals	Pub within walking distance.
Closed	Christmas.
Directions	A44 north from Oxford's ring road. At r'bout, 1 mile before Woodstock, left onto A4095 into Bladon. Last left in village; house on right, on 2nd bend in road, with iron railings.

Helen Stevenson
Manor Road, Bladon, Woodstock OX20 1RU

Tel	+44 (0)1993 812168
Web	www.oxtowns.co.uk/woodstock/manor-farmhouse/

Kings Arms Hotel

Standing proud in historic Woodstock, a refuge from town bustle. Tradition can be found in the classic bar – all boarded floors and leather banquettes – then it's through to the chic, atrium'd dining room with chequered floor, open fire, high-backed chairs and gilded mirrors. Equally up-to-date are the menus: braised lamb shank with rosemary mash, apple brûlée with stem ginger ice cream. Lovely bedrooms of all sizes ramble over two floors: low-slung solid-wood beds, richly coloured throws, super bathrooms with Molten Brown potions. The staff are great, and Blenheim Palace is just around the corner. *No under-12's overnight.*

Price	From £140. Singles from £75.
Rooms	15: 14 doubles, 1 twin.
Meals	Lunch & dinner from £9.95.
Closed	Never.
Directions	On A44 at corner of Market Street in town centre.

David & Sara Sykes
19 Market Street, Woodstock OX20 1SU
Tel   +44 (0)1993 813636
Web   www.kings-hotel-woodstock.co.uk

Caswell House

A handsome 15th-century manor house with an ancient orchard, walled gardens, smooth lawns and a moat brimming with trout. A flagstoned hall leads to a warm sitting room with vast fireplaces and squishy sofas. Spoil yourself in comfortable bedrooms, most with new shower rooms, thick towels, bathroom treats and gorgeous views of the garden through leaded windows. Amanda and Richard are generous and easy-going – a game of snooker is a must! – and seasonal produce is sourced from the farm shop and cooked (deliciously) on the Aga. For heartier souls there are 450 acres of rolling farmland. *Self-catering in Coach House.*

Price	£85. Singles £65.
Rooms	3: 2 doubles, 1 twin/double.
Meals	Pubs/restaurants nearby.
Closed	Rarely.
Directions	A40 Burford to Oxford. Right after 1.8 miles dir. Brize Norton, left at staggered x-roads. Right then left at r'bouts; on for 1.2 miles, house on right.

Kate Matthews
Caswell Lane, Brize Norton OX18 3NJ

Tel	+44 (0)1993 701064
Web	www.caswell-house.co.uk

The Swan

This ancient pub sits in glorious country with the river Windrush passing yards from the front door and a cricket pitch beyond. Interiors come laden with period charm: beautiful windows, open fires, the odd beam. Over the years thirsty feet have worn grooves into 400-year-old flagstones, so follow in their footsteps and stop for a pint of Hook Norton at the bar, then eat from a seasonal menu that brims with local produce. Bedrooms in the old forge are the most recent addition: expect 15th-century walls and 21st-century design. You get pastel colours, smart white linen on comfy beds and a pink chaise longue in the suite.

Price	£110–£180. Singles from £70.
Rooms	6: 4 doubles, 1 twin, 1 suite.
Meals	Main courses £10.95–£17.50; sandwiches (lunch) from £5.25; Sunday roast £13.95.
Closed	Never
Directions	From Oxford A40, through Witney. Village signed right, off A40.

Archie & Nicola Orr-Ewing
Swinbrook, Burford OX18 4DY

Tel	+44 (0)1993 823339
Web	www.theswanswinbrook.co.uk

Burford House

Burford was made rich by 14th-century mill owners. On its high street stands this timber-framed house, its interiors sweeping you back to the elegance of old England: a couple of cosy sitting rooms, a fire that roars, walking maps in the bookcase, a courtyard for summer dining. Slip into the restaurant for rugs on wooden floors, Farrow & Ball colours, freshly cut flowers. Bedrooms are delightful, two across the courtyard. Some have oak beams, others a claw-foot bath, all come with robes in bathrooms and those at the back have rooftop views. Wake on Sunday to the sound of pealing bells. *Minimum stay two nights at weekends.*

Price	£145–£185. Singles from £115.
Rooms	8: 3 doubles, 2 twins/doubles, 3 four-posters.
Meals	Light lunch from £4.95 (not Sundays). Dinner (Thurs-Sat) about £35.
Closed	Rarely.
Directions	In centre of Burford, halfway down hill. Free on-street parking, free public car park nearby.

Ian Hawkins & Stewart Dunkley
99 High Street, Burford OX18 4QA

Tel	+44 (0)1993 823151
Web	www.burfordhouse.co.uk

The Swan at Ascott

Locals are drawn to the bar for the welcome, the wood-burner and the pints of real ale, while the menu draws foodies from afar. Walkers enjoy ciabatta sandwiches and the ploughman's – a deli-board laden with cheese, roast ham, egg, coleslaw, fresh leaves and pickles. Peek at the rooms – four upstairs – and you'll have to stay the night... beautifully revamped in contemporary style they have designer fabrics, sleigh beds and crisp linen, colourful throws, modern prints and fat lamps. One room, under the eaves, has a romantic bed and a bath behind standing timbers. Wake to a hearty breakfast, then explore the Evenlode Valley.

Price	£75–£125.
Rooms	5: 4 doubles, 1 twin.
Meals	Main courses £8.50–£15.95.
Closed	Christmas Day.
Directions	Village and pub signposted off A361 south of Chipping Norton.

Richard Lait
4 Shipton Road, Ascott under Wychwood,
Chipping Norton OX7 6AY

Tel	+44 (0)1993 832332
Web	www.swanatascott.com

Entry 78 Map 4

The Kings Head Inn

Pretty cottages around a village green with quacking ducks, a pond and a perfect pub with a cobbled courtyard. Archie is young, affable and charming with locals and guests; Nic has done up the bedrooms and they look fabulous. All are different, most have family furniture mixed in with 'bits' she's picked up, painted wood, great colours and lush fabrics. The bar is lively; choose rooms over the courtyard if you prefer. Breakfast and supper are taken in the pretty flagstoned dining room, and you can lunch by the fire. Expect delicious puds, serious cheeses, and lovely unpompous touches like jugs of cow parsley in the loo.

Price	£80–£125. Singles from £60.
Rooms	12: 10 doubles, 2 twins.
Meals	Lunch & dinner £6–£30.
Closed	Christmas Day & Boxing Day.
Directions	East out of Stow-on-the-Wold on A436, then right onto B4450 for Bledington. Pub in village on green.

Archie & Nicola Orr-Ewing
The Green, Bledington, Chipping Norton OX7 6XQ
Tel   +44 (0)1608 658365
Web   www.kingsheadinn.net

The Kingham Plough

Emily, once junior sous chef at the famous Fat Duck in Bray, is now doing her own thing: the very best of rustic British. You eat in the tithe barn, now an atmospheric dining room, with ceilings open to ancient rafters and excellent art on the walls. There's a piano by the fire in the locals' bar, a terrace outside for summer dining, fruit trees, herbs and lavender in the garden. Bedrooms, three of which are small, have honest prices and come with super-comfy beds, smart carpets, white linen, the odd beam; one has a claw-foot bath. Arrive by train from London, to be met by a bus that delivers you to the front door. Wonderful.

Price	£85–£125. Singles from £70.
Rooms	7 twins/doubles.
Meals	Lunch from £10. Dinner, 3 courses, about £30.
Closed	Christmas Day.
Directions	Off B4450 between Chipping Norton & Stow-on-the-Wold, signed.

Emily Watkins & Miles Lampson
The Green, Kingham, Chipping Norton OX7 6YD

Tel +44 (0)1608 658327
Web www.thekinghamplough.co.uk

Entry 80 Map 4

Rectory Farm

A general sense of peaceful order pervades at this solid, big house set in a manicured lawn. Inside find large, light bedrooms, floral and feminine, with bold chintz bed covers, draped kidney-shaped dressing tables, thick mattresses; some have garden views, others face the farm buildings. Sink into comfy sofas flanking a huge fireplace in the drawing room, breakfast on local bacon and sausage with free-range eggs, stroll the pretty garden, or grab a rod and try your luck on one of the trout lakes. Elizabeth knows her patch well; walkers can borrow maps, and she can point the way to lovely shops for the dedicated.

Price	£80–£90. Singles £50–£65.
Rooms	3: 1 double, 1 twin/double; 1 twin/double with separate bath.
Meals	Pub/restaurant 1.5 miles.
Closed	December & January.
Directions	A44 from Chipping Norton for Moreton-in-Marsh. After 1.5 miles right into Salford. Right at pub, immed. left uphill past green on right. Left into drive for Rectory Farm, on for 200 yds then left.

Elizabeth Colston
Salford, Chipping Norton OX7 5YZ

Tel	+44 (0)1608 643209
Web	www.rectoryfarm.info

Falkland Arms

In a perfect Cotswold village, the perfect English pub. The fire still roars in the stone-flagged bar under a low timbered ceiling that drips with tankards and mugs. Tradition runs deep; they stock endless tins of snuff and in summer Morris Men jingle in the lane outside. This lively pub is down-to-earth and in very good hands: dig into baked Camembert or plates of charcuterie in the lovely big garden or hop next door to the tiny dining room for home-cooked delights. Bedrooms are cosy, some verging on snug; brass beds and four-posters, maybe a bit of old oak or a creaky floor. Very special, book early for weekends.

Price	£85–£115.
Rooms	5 doubles.
Meals	Main courses £8–£15. Must book for dinner.
Closed	Rarely.
Directions	North from Chipping Norton on A361, then right onto B4022, signed Great Tew. Inn by village green.

Paula & James Meredith
19-21 The Green, Great Tew,
Chipping Norton OX7 4DB

Tel	+44 (0)1608 683653
Web	www.falklandarms.co.uk

Entry 82 Map 4

The Old Post House

Great natural charm in the 17th-century Old Post House, where shiny flagstones, rich dark wood and mullion windows combine with warm fabrics, deep sofas and handsome furniture. Bedrooms are big, with antique wardrobes, oak headboards and a comforting old-fashioned feel. The walled gardens are lovely – rich with espaliered fruit trees, and with a pool for sunny evenings. Christine, a well-travelled ex-pat, has a Springer spaniel and an innate sense of hospitality; her breakfasts are delicious. There's village traffic but your sleep should be sound, and Deddington is delightful. *Children over 12 welcome.*

Price	£80. Singles £52.
Rooms	3: 1 twin/double; 1 double with separate bath, 1 four-poster with separate shower.
Meals	Occasional dinner. Pubs/restaurants in village.
Closed	Rarely.
Directions	A4260 Oxford to Banbury. In Deddington, on right next to cream Georgian house. Park opposite.

Christine Blenntoft
New Street, Deddington OX15 0SP

Tel	+44 (0)1869 338978
Web	www.oldposthouse.co.uk

Home Farmhouse

The house is charming, with low, wobbly ceilings, beams, Inglenook fireplaces and winding stairs; the bedrooms, perched above their own staircases like crows' nests, are traditionally furnished and decorated with swathes of flowery chintz. All rooms are faded and full of character; bathrooms are old fashioned and floral curtains embellish one bath. The barn room has a mixture of furniture and its own entrance up old stone steps. The family's travels are evident all over; this super couple run their B&B as a team. Delightful dogs, too – Samson and Goliath. It's all so laid-back you'll find it hard to leave.

Price	£80. Singles £52.
Rooms	3: 1 double,1 twin/double. Barn: 1 twin/double.
Meals	Dinner £27. Supper £18. Pub 100 yds.
Closed	Christmas.
Directions	M40 Junc. 10, A43 for Northampton. After 5 miles, left to Charlton. There, left & house on left, 100 yds past Rose & Crown.

Rosemary & Nigel Grove-White
Charlton, Banbury OX17 3DR

Tel	+44 (0)1295 811683
Web	www.homefarmhouse.co.uk

Uplands House

Come to be spoiled at this 'farmhouse' built in 1875 for the Earl of Jersey's son. Renovated by a talented couple, it's elegant and sumptuously furnished; expect large light bedrooms, crisp linen, thick towels and long bucolic views from the Orangery where you have tea and cake. Relax here with a book as the sounds and scents of the pretty garden waft by, or chat to charming Poppy while she creates delicious dinner – a convivial occasion enjoyed with your hosts. Breakfast is Graham's domain – try smoked salmon with scrambled eggs and red caviar. You're well placed for exploring but you'll find it hard to leave.

Price	£90-£150. Singles £60-£90.
Rooms	3: 1 double; 1 twin/double, 1 four-poster each with separate bath.
Meals	Dinner, 2-4 courses, £20-£30. Pub 1.25 miles.
Closed	Rarely.
Directions	M40 junc.11; thro' Banbury, A422 towards Stratford. Thro' Wroxton; just after 'Upton House' National Trust sign, right single lane drive marked 'Uplands Farm'. 1st drive on right to house.

Poppy Cooksey & Graham Paul
Upton, Banbury OX15 6HJ

Tel	+44 (0)1295 678663
Web	www.cotswolds-uplands.co.uk

Gower's Close

All the nooks, crannies and beams you'd expect from an ancient thatched cottage in a Cotswold village… and more besides: good food, lively conversation and lots of inside information about gardens to visit. Judith is a keen gardener who writes books on the subject (her passion for plants is evident from her own glorious garden) and her style and intelligence are reflected in her home. Pretty, south-facing and full of sunlight, the sitting room opens onto the garden and terrace. Bedrooms are light, charming and cottagey – the twin is at garden level. A thoroughly relaxing place to stay.

Price	£75. Singles £50.
Rooms	2: 1 double, 1 twin.
Meals	Dinner, 4 courses, £28 (min. 4 people). Pub/restaurant 100 yds.
Closed	Christmas & New Year.
Directions	In Sibford Gower, 0.5 miles south off B4035 between Banbury & Chipping Campden. House on Main Street, same side as church & school.

Judith Hitching & John Marshall
Sibford Gower, Banbury OX15 5RW

Tel	+44 (0)1295 780348
Web	www.gowersclose.co.uk

Buttslade House

Choose between a gorgeous ground-floor retreat across the courtyard, or a very pretty room in the 17th-century farmhouse with its barns and stables. Both have their own sitting rooms with a clever melody of ancient and contemporary styles; Spanish art, antique sofas, bright cushions. Beds have seriously good mattresses, feather and down pillows and crisp white linen; bathrooms are smart and sparkling – one with a Victorian roll top. Diana is lovely, and will pamper you or leave you, there's a blissful garden to stroll through, food is fresh and local and it's a hop to the village pub. A fun and stylish treat.

Price	£75. Singles £50.
Rooms	2: 1 double & sitting room; 1 twin & sitting room with separate bath.
Meals	Dinner, 3 courses, £25. Lunch £7. Pub 100 yds.
Closed	Rarely.
Directions	From B4035 look for signs to Wykham Arms. Buttslade is 2nd house beyond pub, going down the hill.

Diana Thompson
Temple Mill Road, Sibford Gower,
Banbury OX15 5RX

Tel   +44 (0)1295 788818
Web   www.buttsladehouse.co.uk

Minehill House

Bump your way up the track (mind the car!) to the top of a wild and windswept hill and a gorgeous family farmhouse with views for miles and young, energetic Hester to care for you. Children will adore the ping-pong table and the trampoline; their parents will enjoy the gleaming old flagstones, vibrant contemporary oils, wood-burning stove and seriously sophisticated food. Rest well in the big double room with its verdant leafy wallpaper and stunning views, and a cubby-hole door to extra twin beds; bathrooms are sparklingly clean and spacious. All this, and bracing walks straight from the door.

Price	£90. Singles from £50.
Rooms	1 double/family.
Meals	Dinner, 3 courses, £30. Supper £15. BYO. Packed lunch available. Pubs 1-5 miles.
Closed	Christmas & New Year.
Directions	From Banbury B4035 to Brailes; after 10 miles take road left signed Hook Norton; 0.5 miles, right onto unmarked uphill farm track to house.

Hester & Ed Sale
Lower Brailes, Banbury OX15 5BJ

Tel   +44 (0)1608 685594

The Red Lion

Dogs are welcome in this ancient warren of a pub; the pub's own, Cocoa 'The Landlady', is often around. But that doesn't mean the whiff of wet canine. Instead you will get the mouthwatering aroma of excellent cooking from Sarah Keightley, co-manager and chef. And you can stay, in five rooms that reflect the unfussy approach. With natural colours and crisp ginghams, their comfort makes up for their size (in a place that goes back 250 years, bedrooms are not likely to be huge). Downstairs there's space for everyone, from the pool room to the flagged bar area warmed by a real fire. A smart village pub full of character.

Price	£80–£110. Singles £55.
Rooms	5: 2 doubles, 1 twin, 1 single, 1 family room.
Meals	Main courses £10.50–£17.95
Closed	Never.
Directions	Beside A3400 between Chipping Norton & Shipston-on-Stour.

Lisa Phipps & Sarah Keightley
Main Street, Long Compton,
Shipston-on-Stour CV36 5JS

Entry 89 Map 4

Tel   +44 (0)1608 684221
Web   www.redlion-longcompton.co.uk

The Howard Arms

Standing on Ilmington Green, five miles south of Stratford-upon-Avon, the inn is as old as Shakespeare. Little has changed – flagstones, beams, mellow stone walls, glowing logs in a vast open fire. Now a blackboard menu scales the wall, there are oils on walls, books on shelves, maps for walkers and an elegant dining room with arched windows that overlook the green; dig in to beef and ale pie, spicy pear and apple crumble. Three gorgeous bedrooms in the main house mix period style with modern luxury, while five new garden rooms come in elegant contemporary style with fancy bathrooms. *Minimum stay two nights at weekends.*

Price	£120–£150. Singles from £90.
Rooms	8: 5 doubles, 1 twin, 2 twins/doubles.
Meals	Lunch from £5. Dinner, 3 courses, about £25.
Closed	Never.
Directions	From Stratford, south on A3400 for 4 miles, right to Wimpstone & Ilmington. Pub in village centre.

Tim Churchman
Lower Green, Ilmington,
Shipston-on-Stour CV36 4LT

Tel   +44 (0)1608 682226
Web   www.howardarms.com

Old Manor Cottage

This clematis-swathed thatched cottage has bright, uneven 18th-century walls, painted beams and paned windows. There's a hint of Scandinavia in your little kitchen with its glass table, stylish scoop chairs and heated flagged floors, and in the cosy sitting room with red striped and white cotton armchairs, crisp floral curtains and an open fire. Head up steep stairs past a little bed tucked under a window to a pitched roof main bedroom with simple cream furniture and a new bed wrapped in white cotton. In the scented peace of the owner's much loved rose borders overlooking the orchard, this is the essence of peaceful village life.

Price	£350–£550 per week.
Rooms	Cottage for 3 (4 with sofabed): 1 double, 1 single.
Meals	Self-catering.
Closed	Rarely.
Directions	Given on booking.

Jane Pusey
Halford, Shipston-on-Stour CV36 5BT

Tel +44 (0)1789 740264
Web www.oldmanor-cottage.co.uk

The Old Manor House

An attractive 16th-century manor house with beautiful landscaped gardens sweeping down to the river Stour. The beamed double has oak furniture and a big bathroom; the old-fashioned twin and single are in a private wing. There is a large and elegant drawing and dining room whose antiques, contemporary art and open fire are for visitors to share. Jane prepares first-class breakfasts, and in warm weather you can have tea on the terrace: pots of tulips in spring, old scented roses in summer, meadow land beyond. A comfortable, lived-in family house with Stratford and the theatre close by. *Children over seven welcome.*

Price	£85–£90. Singles from £50.
Rooms	3: 1 double with separate bath; 1 twin, 1 single sharing bath (2nd room let to same party only).
Meals	Restaurants nearby.
Closed	Rarely.
Directions	From Stratford, A422 for 4 miles for Banbury. After 4 miles, right at r'bout onto A429 for Halford. There, 1st right, down hill on Queen's Street. House straight ahead after 150 yds.

Jane Pusey
Halford, Shipston-on-Stour CV36 5BT

Tel	+44 (0)1789 740264
Web	www.oldmanor-halford.co.uk

Entry 92 Map 4

Oxbourne House

Hard to believe the house is new, with its beamed ceilings, fireplaces and antiques. Bedrooms are fresh, crisp, cosy and cared for, the family room with an 'in the attic' feel; lighting is soft, beds excellent, bath and shower rooms attractive and warm, and views far-reaching. In the garden are tennis, sculpture and Graeme's rambler-bedecked pergola. Wake to birdsong and fresh eggs from their own hens; on peaceful summer nights, watch the dipping sun. Posy and Graeme are hugely likeable and welcoming and the delightful village pub is just down the road. A most comforting place to stay. *Dogs by arrangement.*

Price	£65–£85. Singles from £45.
Rooms	3: 1 double, 1 family room; 1 twin/double with separate bath.
Meals	Dinner from £20. Pub 2-minute walk.
Closed	Rarely.
Directions	A422 from Stratford-upon-Avon for Banbury. After 8 miles, right to Oxhill. Last house on right on Whatcote Road.

Graeme & Posy McDonald
Oxhill, Warwick CV35 0RA

Tel	+44 (0)1295 688202
Web	www.oxbournehouse.com

Red House Barn

A fresh and funky spot, just for two. Sallie has poured love into this project, and her vivacious personality shines through; there are books and pretty fabrics and art, old and new, on the walls. Once a stable block, this space has been converted with sleeping and living rolled into one. A fat sofa lines one wall, the splendid bed with its marshmallow pillows is against another, all is under wooden beams. The sparkling kitchen has a breakfast bar with a view; a weeping willow tickles the lawn in the shared garden. The position couldn't be better: Stratford-upon-Avon and a host of National Trust gardens are a short drive.

Price	£290–£390 per week. Short breaks from £180.
Rooms	Barn for 2: 1 double with bath/shower.
Meals	Self-catering.
Closed	Never.
Directions	Given on booklng.

Sallie Button
Red House, Kineton, Warwick CV35 0JH
Tel   +44 (0)1926 642445
Web   www.redhousebarn.org

Fulready Manor

Fulready is majestic, a castle in the fields, with soothing views at the back over lamb-dotted fields to rippling hills. There's a lake, too, with a rowing boat for excursions to the island. All this you gaze upon dreamily from a glorious drawing room (muralled walls, huge sofas, mullioned windows). Bedrooms are just as you'd expect, with Sanderson wallpapers, thick fabrics, mahogany furniture, perhaps an old oak four-poster; one room has a sitting room in a turret. Best of all are Michael and Mauveen who pamper you in best B&B fashion with grilled grapefruits and home-laid eggs among myriad breakfast treats. *No credit cards.*

Price	£125–£140.
Rooms	3: 1 double, 2 four-posters.
Meals	Restaurants within 5 miles.
Closed	Christmas & New Year.
Directions	M40 junc. 11, then A422 west. Left in Pillerton Priors (B4451). Fulready first driveway on left after 0.25 miles.

Michael & Mauveen Spencer
Fulready, Ettington,
Stratford-upon-Avon CV37 7PE

Tel	+44 (0)1789 740152
Web	www.fulreadymanor.co.uk

The Bakehouse

Red-bricked and mellow on the outside, a lavishly romantic bolt-hole within. Find a rose-soft sofa laden with tapestry cushions, an embellished repro mirror with a fun French flourish, plentiful glossy mags and little gilt-framed pictures, and a wood-burner that belts out the heat... and that's just the sitting room! The bedroom is spacious and light, with immaculate carpeting, dark beams and a view onto the neighbouring farmyard and gardens. There's a tiny furnished courtyard for guests and Shoshana leaves a continental breakfast in your well-equipped kitchen. Comfort, character and style, minutes from Stratford and its theatres.

Price	From £70.
Rooms	1 double (extra single available).
Meals	Restaurant/pub next door.
Closed	Never.
Directions	From Stratford-upon-Avon, Shipston road then right to Broadway B4632 for 3 miles. Signed Lower Quinton on left.

Shoshana Kitchen
Magdalen House, The Green, Lower Quinton,
Stratford-upon-Avon CV37 8SG

Tel	+44 (0)1789 721792
Web	www.cotswoldbakehouse.co.uk

Cross o' th' Hill Farm

Stratford in 12 minutes on foot, down a footpath across a field: from the veranda you can see the church where Shakespeare is buried. There's been a farm on this rural spot since before Shakespeare's time but part of the house is Victorian. Built around 1860, it's full of light, with wall-to-ceiling sash windows, glass panelling in the roof, large uncluttered bedrooms and smart, newly decorated bathrooms. The garden, full of trees and birds, dates from the same period – there's even a sunken croquet lawn. Decima grew up here; she and David are gentle hosts, and passionate about art and architecture.

Price	£90–£95. Singles £65–£70.
Rooms	3: 2 doubles; 1 double with separate shower/bathroom.
Meals	Pubs/restaurants 20-minute walk.
Closed	20 December–1 March.
Directions	From Stratford south on A3400 for 0.5 miles, 2nd right on B4632 for Broadway Rd for 500 yds. 2nd drive on right for farm.

Decima Noble
Broadway Road, Stratford-upon-Avon
CV37 8HP

Tel	+44 (0)1789 204738
Web	www.crossothhillfarm.com

Sequoia House

A cat snoozes by the Aga in this smart Victorian townhouse – an easy stroll from Stratford and a civilised base for exploring Shakespeare country. Step into a pretty tiled hallway and discover high ceilings, deep bays, generous landings, handsome flagstones, a homely sitting room. The easygoing Evanses (Welsh-born) downsized from the hotel they used to run here and are happy to treat just a few guests: trouser presses and piles of towels mingle with fine old furniture in immaculate rooms. A walkway runs past cricket grounds straight into town. Hotel touches but a warmly personal welcome, and so wonderfully convenient.

Price	£125. Singles £85.
Rooms	6 doubles.
Meals	Pub/restaurant 100 yds.
Closed	Christmas & New Year.
Directions	From north and M40 (junc. 15) to Stratford. Enter town, follow signs A3400 Shipston. Cross River Bridge, then 2nd exit off traffic island. House 100 yds on left. From south, join A3400 and enter Stratford. House on left 100 yds before traffic island.

Jean Evans
51 Shipston Road, Stratford-upon-Avon
CV37 7LN

Tel	+44 (0)1789 268852	Entry 98 Map 4
Web	www.sequoia-house.co.uk	

Rydal Cottage

Shakespeare was born down the road from this sweet cottage. Step straight into the kitchen, immediately welcoming with its slate floor, stainless-steel range and rose-pink café table. When the sun's out, head to the little paved back garden, fire up the barbecue and dine under a big umbrella. The living room is spotless and soft-carpeted; the beauty of this place is its spick and span simplicity. Upstairs are two restful doubles, one street-side, the other overlooking the garden; both share a ground-floor bathroom with a roll top bath. Hop in the car to explore the region's castles, cities and towns; Oxford is 30 miles away.

Price	£375–£700 per week.
Rooms	Cottage for 4: 2 doubles.
Meals	Self-catering.
Closed	Never.
Directions	Given on booking.

Fay Frampton
9 Great William St, Stratford-upon-Avon CV37 6RY
Tel   +44 (0)7765 573428
Web   www.stratford-selfcatering.co.uk

Salford Farm House

Beautiful within, handsome without. Thanks to subtle colours, oak beams and lovely old pieces, Jane has achieved a seductive combination of comfort and style. A flagstoned hallway and an old rocking horse, ticking clocks, beeswax, fresh flowers: the house is well-loved. Jane was a ballet dancer and Richard has green fingers and runs a fruit farm nearby – you may expect meat and game from the Ragley Estate and delicious fruits in season. Bedrooms have a soft, warm elegance and flat-screen TVs, bathrooms are spotless and welcoming, views are to garden or fields. Wholly delightful.

Price	£85. Singles £52.50.
Rooms	2 twins/doubles.
Meals	Dinner £25. Restaurant 2.5 miles.
Closed	Rarely.
Directions	A46 from Evesham or Stratford; exit for Salford Priors. On entering village, right opp. church, for Dunnington. House on right, approx. 1 mile on, after 2nd sign on right for Dunnington.

Jane & Richard Beach
Salford Priors, Evesham WR11 8XN

Tel	+44 (0)1386 870000
Web	www.salfordfarmhouse.co.uk

Alcombe Manor

Down a maze of magical lanes discover this hamlet and its 17th-century manor house: a deeply romantic hideaway with panelling, wooden floors, a couple of medieval windows, deep sofas, log fires, a galleried hall, shelves of books and plenty of places to sit. A fine oak staircase leads to large, light bedrooms, reassuringly old-fashioned; carpeted floors creak companionably and every ancient leaded window has a dreamy garden view... five acres of English perfection, no less, with topiary and a stream dashing through. Your hosts are kind and helpful, the peace is palpable, and you are just five miles from Bath.

Price	From £80. Singles £50.
Rooms	3: 2 twins, each with separate bath/shower; 1 single sharing bath.
Meals	Occasional dinner. Pubs nearby.
Closed	Rarely.
Directions	M4 junc. 17; A4 to Bath through Box; right for Middle Hill & Ditteridge; 200 yds, left signed Alcombe. Up hill for 0.5 miles, fork right; 200 yds on left.

Simon & Victoria Morley
Box, Corsham SN13 8QQ

Tel +44 (0)1225 743850

The Coach House

In an ancient hamlet a few miles north of Bath, an impeccable conversion of an early 19th-century barn. Bedrooms are fresh and cosy with sloping ceilings; the drawing room is elegant with porcelain and chintz, its pale walls the ideal background for striking displays of fresh flowers. Sliding glass doors lead to a south-facing patio... then to a well-groomed croquet lawn bordered by flowers, with vegetable garden, tennis court, woodland and paddock beyond. Helga and David are delightful and there's lots to do from here; the splendours of Bath, Castle Combe and plenty of good golf courses are all near.

Price	£65–£80. Singles from £35.
Rooms	2: 1 double with separate bath/shower; 1 twin/double let to same party only.
Meals	Dinner, 3 courses, from £20. Pubs/restaurants 1 mile.
Closed	Rarely.
Directions	From M4 junc. 17, A350 for Chippenham. A420 to Bristol (east) & Castle Combe. After 6.3 miles, right into Upper Wraxall. Sharp left opp. village green; at end of drive.

Helga & David Venables
Upper North Wraxall, Chippenham SN14 7AG

Tel	+44 (0)1225 891026
Web	www.upperwraxallcoachhouse.co.uk

The Bothy, Sheldon Manor

A stately lime-lined avenue brings you to Sheldon Manor, with its 13th-century porch and 1400s chapel. The last in a line of three soft brick cottages, the Bothy has its own sunken courtyard, perfect for sundowners. Be charmed by mullion windows, polished wood floors, fine furniture, cream bedspreads and fresh touches – and a four-poster dressed in white muslin. Explore the rose garden; help yourself to produce (in season); dip in the pool; return to a light flooded sitting room, cosy with open fireplace and cream sofa. It is elegant but not precious, and perfect for weddings. Cotswold villages are a short drive.

Price	£1,000–£1,250 per week.
Rooms	Cottage for 4: 1 double, 1 four-poster.
Meals	Self-catering.
Closed	Rarely.
Directions	Given on booking.

Caroline Hawkins
Chippenham SN14 0RG

Tel   +44 (0)1249 653120
Web   www.sheldonmanor.co.uk

Barton Place, Sheldon Manor

Wiltshire's oldest inhabited manor house is a beauty. In the renovated stable wing are three cottages, Barton Place being the biggest. Enter a graceful hallway with a leather settle and sprigs of greenery on a polished table. White blinds show off mullion windows, pretty lampshades add colour. There's a small kitchen and a carpeted dining room, a wood-burning stove engulfed in a marble fireplace and soft sofas. Tuck the little ones up in the attic; next door's doubles come with petal-sprinkled towels and a roll top bath. All around is English garden; venture further and you'll find Bath, Cheltenham and Cotswold towns.

Price	£1,000–£1,250 per week.
Rooms	Cottage for 4 (5 with child's bed): 2 doubles.
Meals	Self-catering.
Closed	Rarely.
Directions	Given on booking.

Caroline Hawkins
Chippenham SN14 0RG
Tel   +44 (0)1249 653120
Web   www.sheldonmanor.co.uk

Entry 104 Map 1

The Cockloft, Sheldon Manor

Magical Sheldon: honey-hued and 13th-century. Its chapel is beautiful and the trees in the gardens could have been plucked from a Keatsian poem: medlar and sloe, apple and rose… The first in a row of stone cottages, the Cockloft is light, fresh, quirky and elegant. Character comes from exuberant displays of home-grown flowers, a cowskin rug on a warm brick floor, a wood-burner, window seats, a Knowle sofa. On the mezzanine is the bedroom, seagrass underfoot, striking beams above. Outside: space for a table and chairs, terraced gardens, ancient yews, a romantic love seat and a pool. Bliss on the Cotswolds' fringe.

Price	£600–£760 per week.
Rooms	Cottage for 2: 1 double.
Meals	Self-catering.
Closed	Rarely.
Directions	Given on booking.

Entry 105 Map 1

Caroline Hawkins
Chippenham SN14 0RG
Tel   +44 (0)1249 653120
Web   www.sheldonmanor.co.uk

The Wing, Sheldon Manor

On the edge of the Cotswolds, a Grade I-listed manor house, wrapped in acres of English country garden, with a 15th-century chapel and the oldest stone porch in the country. Nothing is over-embellished, nothing overdone; Caroline and Ken have allowed the house's beauty to shine. Slip around the side, past the medieval grain-store, and step straight in to The Wing. Light floods in through mullion windows, there's a big sofa in front of the wood-burner and lovely bedrooms above, with coir carpeting and the odd floral touch. Explore the rose gardens, the orchard, swim in the pool. Heaven, 70 minutes from London.

Price	£1,300–£1,600 per week.
Rooms	Wing for 6: 3 doubles.
Meals	Pubs/restaurants 3 miles.
Closed	Rarely.
Directions	Given on booking.

	Caroline Hawkins
	Chippenham SN14 0RG
Tel	+44 (0)1249 653120
Web	www.sheldonmanor.co.uk

Church Farm Cottage

No madding crowds in Kington Langley – one reason why Kate and Will fell for this cluster of pretty 18th-century farm buildings. Step into a light open sitting and dining room, decked out with quirky antique pieces (some for sale once you've tried them!). Easy to rustle up a Sunday roast in the fitted kitchen with its unusual jigsaw pattern floors. Upstairs, slip back in time as you recline on a scroll-ended settee or curl up on a brass four-poster. Outside the dreamy theme continues, with pecking hens and grazing sheep beyond an organic kitchen garden and living willow fence; a bluebell woodland walk is to follow.

Price	£360–£520 per week.
Rooms	Cottage for 2 (4 with extra beds): 1 double.
Meals	Self-catering.
Closed	Never.
Directions	Given on booking.

William and Kate Bicknell
Church Farm, Middle Common,
Kington Langley, Chippenham SN15 5NN

Tel   +44 (0)1249 750264
Web   www.churchfarmuk.com

Mead Cottage

A listed stone cottage in an idyllic setting – and you can pick up the phone and order bacon sarnies and champagne! The owner has a deal with The Manor House Hotel, so room service is yours for the asking. Contemporary bedrooms ooze feather down pillows and cotton chambray; white baths (one in a bedroom) stand on heated floors; and the kitchen will satisfy the most exacting of chefs. Plus a chic dining room in the cellar, a modish living room and a sun-trap terrace. Golfers, equestrians (Badminton) and lovers of historic properties will think they've gone to heaven. *Two parking spaces available at neighbouring hotel.*

Price	£718-£1,100 per week.
Rooms	Cottage for 4: 1 double with bath, 1 twin/double.
Meals	Self-catering.
Closed	Never.
Directions	Given on booking.

Joanna Broughton
4 West Street, Castle Combe,
Chippenham SN14 7HP

Tel	+44 (0)7775 584329
Web	www.meadcottage.com

Manor Farm

Farmyard heaven in the Cotswolds. A 17th-century farmhouse in 550 arable acres; horses in the paddock, dozing dogs in the yard, tumbling blooms at the door and a perfectly tended village, replete with duck pond, a short walk. Beautiful bedrooms are softly lit, with muted colours, goose down pillows and the crispest linen. Breakfast in front of the fire is a banquet of delights, tea among the roses is a treat, thanks to charming, welcoming Victoria. This is the postcard England of dreams, with Castle Combe, Lacock, grand walking and gardens to visit. "The perfect place for a break," says a reader. *Children over 12 welcome.*

Price	From £80. Singles from £43.
Rooms	3: 2 doubles; 1 twin with separate bath.
Meals	Pub 1 mile. Wild venison suppers by arrangement.
Closed	Rarely.
Directions	From M4 A429 to Cirencester (junc. 17). After 200 yds, 1st left for Grittleton; there, follow signs to Alderton. Farmhouse near church.

Victoria Lippiatt-Onslow
Alderton, Chippenham SN14 6NL

Tel   +44 (0)1666 840271
Web   www.themanorfarm.co.uk

Manor Farm

The road through the sleepy Wiltshire village brings you to a Queen Anne house with a *petit château* feel, enfolded by a tranquil garden with tulip meadow, groomed lawns and... hens! Inside is as lovely; watercolourist Clare is a perfectionist behind the scenes and is charming. The bedroom is elegant and cosy, its soft-painted panelled walls hung with good pictures, its sash windows beautifully dressed. Scrumptious, all-organic breakfasts are served in a butter-yellow kitchen; the eclectically furnished drawing room, shared among guests, has a real fire and a delightful lived-in, family feel.

Price	£90. Singles by arrangement.
Rooms	1 double.
Meals	Pub 200 yds.
Closed	Christmas & New Year.
Directions	M4 exit 17. North on A429 for Malmesbury, right on B4042. Right after 3 miles to Little Somerford. Past pub, right at crossroads, 50 yds on, house behind tall wall.

Clare Inskip
Little Somerford, Chippenham SN15 5JW
Tel   +44 (0)1666 822140

Smokey Cottage

Super Susie looks after you with delightful ease in her 50s brick and flint house on a quiet country road. Flop in a lovely L-shaped sitting room with lots of pictures of dogs and horses and big windows overlooking the large garden; breakfast here on jolly days. Your bedroom is light, sunny and cosy with birds of paradise swooping over curtains and headboard; books, squishy cushions, bamboo tables and Chinese style lamps give character and your bathroom is functional but spotless. Eat in or walk to the pub; Susie, Dynamite the labrador and Bossy the Jack Russell will welcome you home afterwards.

Price	£70. Singles £50.
Rooms	1 twin/double with separate bath.
Meals	Dinner £25, and contribution for wine. Pub 0.25 miles.
Closed	Christmas & New Year.
Directions	M4 junction 16, then B4042. Through Brinkworth, then left to Somerfords, Clay Street. Left then immediate right, The Street. House 800 yds on right.

Susie Brassey
Little Somerford, Chippenham SN15 5JW
Tel   +44 (0)1666 822255

Manor Farm

Iron gates, a sweeping drive with fountain and lawn to an impressive Cotswold stone house, through an ancient oak door find a large hallway and Caroline who makes you feel truly welcome to roam the house. While away time in the enormous sitting room with its piles of good books, eat breakfast from the local shop in the kitchen – or by the wood-burner in the dining room, sleep in deep comfort and surrounded by beautiful things, wake to a cockerel crowing and church bells: wholly comfortable, deeply unpretentious. You are near to Tetbury for delightfully expensive antiques, and Westonbirt for wood walks. *French spoken.*

Price	£90. Singles £65.
Rooms	2: 1 double, 1 twin with separate shared bath (let to same party only).
Meals	Pub/restaurant 100 yds.
Closed	Christmas & Boxing Day.
Directions	M4 junction 17, north on A429. Left to Hullavington & Sherston. Follow road through to Sherston. Straight over into Court Street. Drive to house on left after 100 yds.

Caroline Marcq
Court Street, Sherston SN16 0LL

Tel   +44 (0)1666 841102

The Horse & Groom Inn

A proper inn, 500 years old, rescued from neglect, now shining brightly. A smart rustic feel runs throughout: exposed stone walls, log fires, the odd beam, candles at night. Smart dining areas – gleaming tables, polished glasses – and bedrooms sparkling with style and panache all await hungry and weary travellers. Delicious country food is served, from Jerusalem artichoke velouté to pub classics. Bedrooms have padded window seats, chunky wood beds, herbal toiletries, earthy colours; those in the eaves have painted beams. Everything is immaculate and there's a secret walled garden for civilised summer drinking. Wonderful.

Price	From £89.
Rooms	5 doubles.
Meals	Lunch from £10. Sunday lunch £14.95-£19.95. Dinner, 3 courses, £25-£30.
Closed	Rarely.
Directions	M4 junc. 17, then A429 north for Cirencester. Right onto B4040 after 5 miles. On left in village after 1 mile.

Entry 113 Map 1

	Dave Whitney-Brown
	The Street, Charlton, Malmesbury SN16 9DL
Tel	+44 (0)1666 823904
Web	www.horseandgroominn.com

Bullocks Horn Cottage

Up a country lane to this hidden-away house which the Legges have turned into a haven of peace and seclusion. Liz loves fabrics and mixes them with flair, Colin has painted a colourful mural – complete with macaws – in the conservatory. Bedrooms are quiet with lovely views, the sitting room with log fire has large comfy sofas, and the garden, which has been featured in various magazines, is exceptional. Home veg and herbs and local seasonal food are used at dinner which, in summer, you can eat in the cool shade of the arbour, covered in climbing roses and jasmine. *Children over 12 welcome.*

Price	From £75. Singles from £40.
Rooms	2: 1 twin; 1 twin with separate bath.
Meals	Dinner £20-£25. BYO. Pub 1.5 miles.
Closed	Christmas.
Directions	From A429, B4040 through Charlton, past Horse & Groom. 0.5 miles, left signed 'Bullocks Horn No Through Road'. On to end of lane. Right then 1st on left.

Colin & Liz Legge
Charlton, Malmesbury SN16 9DZ
Tel   +44 (0)1666 577600
Web   www.bullockshorn.co.uk

The Red Lion Inn

A stroll from the ancient North Meadow, the rambling old coaching inn lies off the Thames path. Revived by the Real Pub Food Company and specialising in seasonal, local and often organic food, it combines contemporary features with a charming 16th-century fabric. In the red-carpeted bar, all low beams and ancient settles, treat yourself to a pint of Ramsbury Gold. Lunches involve the best of English classics; evening dishes, served at wooden tables in the smart new restaurant, include wonderful tea-smoked salmon. The pick of the bedrooms are the two in the stables with their stone walls and hand-crafted beds. Marvellous.

Price	£65.
Rooms	5: 3 doubles, 2 twins.
Meals	Main courses £9.50–£20.95; bar meals £5.50–£10.25; Sunday lunch £13.95 & £16.95.
Closed	Rarely.
Directions	Cricklade is off A417 between Swindon and Cirencester; pub at lower end of High Street.

Tom Gee
74 High Street, Cricklade SN6 6DD
Tel   +44 (0)1793 750776
Web   www.theredlioncricklade.co.uk

Entry 115 Map 2

Westhill House

A large Regency house in the centre of an ancient hilltop market town, just on the edge of the Cotswolds. Vivacious Brenda, well-travelled and a collector of art, has filled her home with bold colours, eclectic paintings, beautiful glass and ceramics; the elegant drawing room has an open fire and the dining room is dramatically red. Bedrooms come in creams and blues, beds are new, wine glasses and cork screw await; bathrooms are contemporary and indulgent with fluffy towels. Be greeted with tea and cake, try French toast with fruit and maple syrup for breakfast or full English. There are marked walking trails from the door.

Price	£75–£105. Singles £60–£90.
Rooms	3 doubles.
Meals	Pubs/restaurants within 5 miles.
Closed	Rarely.
Directions	Exit 15 off M4, A419 to Cirencester. Take A361 Burford, Highworth exit. Left at lights in Highworth onto Cricklade Road. House on right immed. after Oak Drive. Black wrought iron gate.

Brenda Haywood
Cricklade Road, Highworth SN6 7BL

Tel	+44 (0)1793 764219
Web	www.westhillhouse.net

Harrowfields

Tucked just off the high street this compact cottage is massively comfortable and stylish too: contemporary colours and old beams, great books and a homely feel. The bedroom is large enough to lounge in with a good sofa, an antique brass bed, crisp linen and your own cosy wood-burner; in the shower room the spoiling continues – and there are lovely garden views. Susie and Adam (who cooks) are natural and charming, hens cluck around outside, breakfast is local and seasonal, you can walk for miles or just to the pub. Young, romantic couples will be in heaven here; uncork the wine, light the fire, turn up the music.

Price	£70. Singles from £50.
Rooms	1 double.
Meals	Pubs in village.
Closed	Rarely.
Directions	Enter Eckington from Bredon (M5 junc. 9). Turn 1st right by village shop. House on left before Anchor pub.

Entry 117 Map 3

Susie Alington & Adam Stanford
Cotheridge Lane, Eckington WR10 3BA
Tel +44 (0)1386 751053
Web www.harrowfields.co.uk

The King's Arms Inn

The roadside village inn sports slate floors, oak settles in the bar, and a cheekily bright front room adorned with lithographs of the area. In the dining room are terracotta walls, chunky wooden tables and high-backed chairs. There's a big fireplace for winter, darts and dominoes, a walled garden for summer, delicious daily-changing menus and a sign that reads, 'If they don't serve beer in heaven, then I'm not going'. Rooms upstairs, the quietest at the back, are cosy and inviting, with colourful throws on comfortable beds and spotless shower rooms; the self-catering cottages are in the coaching stable.

Price	£75. Single from £55. Cottages from £90.
Rooms	4 + 3: 1 double, 2 twins/doubles, 1 single. 3 self-catering cottages (2 for 4, 1 for 6).
Meals	Main courses £8.95-£16.95; bar meals £4.95-£9.95.
Closed	Never.
Directions	M4 junc. 18, A46 north, then A433 for Tetbury. In village on left.

Alastair & Sarah Sadler
The Street, Didmarton, Badminton GL9 1DT

Tel   +44 (0)1454 238245
Web   www.kingsarmsdidmarton.co.uk

Fires, flagstones, settles and bags of style, regional recipes and artisan produce, gardens to chill out in, pork scratchings by the bar and, of course, great beer. Here's our pick of the Cotswolds' pubs.

The Tunnel House Inn, Coates, Cirencester, GL7 6PW

A gracious Cotswold stone house by the Severn & Thames Canal, with a big garden and open-field views. Enjoy the laid-back hospitality, the beef and horseradish sandwiches, the scrubbed tables, the big faded sofas in front of the fire, the Uley Bitter and the many wines by the glass.

The Marlborough Tavern, 35 Marlborough Buildings, Bath, BA1 2LY

An airy, friendly room with a central bar, sage green paintwork, velvety wallpapers, sofas and village hall furniture - and you can sip from a fashionable palette of rosés in the garden. Fish arrives daily from Cornwall and Devon, Sunday lunches are the stuff of legend and booking is pretty much essential.

The Potting Shed Pub, Crudwell, Malmesbury, SN16 9EW

Open fireplaces and stylish kilim sofas, old butchers' block tables and mix 'n' match antiques: an airy, quirky décor. The food is exuberantly British, from the battered hake to the rabbit terrine, the good children's menu and the puds to warm your heart. Dog biscuits on the bar reflect the focus on real-pub values; 21st-century pub heaven.

The Swan at Southrop, Southrop, Lechlade, GL7 3NU

A roaring log fire, a sober décor, a relaxed mood and a skittle alley for locals – it's the village inn on the village green that everyone dreams of. Menus are seasonal and unshowy (a crab, saffron and tomato tart, roast rump of Southrop lamb), excellent wines match flavoursome ales, and faultless service comes with a big smile.

Seven Tuns Inn, Queen Street, Chedworth, Cheltenham, GL54 4AE
Part-creepered on the outside, the village pub rambles attractively inside, past open fires, aged furniture and a skittle alley with darts. After a gentle walk to Chedworth's Roman Villa, there's no finer place to return to for a pint of Young's Bitter. Mingle with cyclists and locals in the little lounge or rustic bar; if you're here to eat you overlook the garden through mullioned windows.

The Old Spot, 2 Hill Road, Dursley, GL11 4JQ
Ale buffs make pilgrimages to sample the brews; real ciders include Weston's and Ashton Press. For a pub named after a rare-breed pig it's no surprise there are porcine figurines all over the place. Food is simple and pubby – BLT sandwiches, bangers and mash, home-baked pies with shortcrust pastry lids. Friendly, traditional and on the Cotswolds Way.

The Old Green Tree, 12 Green Street, Bath, BA1 2JZ
In the centre of Bath, the cosy pub, whose staff are fanatical about ale, hums with life even before midday. Undecorated since the panelling was installed in 1928, the pub is part of our heritage and has no intention of changing. There are three little, low-ceilinged rooms, the menu includes hearty old English dishes, and drink is not limited to beer: there are malts, wines and hot toddies.

The Rose & Crown, Shilton, Burford, OX18 4AB
In a mellow Cotswold village, the 16th-century Rose & Crown holds just two rooms: the tiny bar itself, and a fractionally larger extension built in 1701. An open fire in the inglenook, a medley of kitchen tables and chairs, beams, fresh flowers, Old Hooky on tap, and, if you're lucky, roast partridge with blackberries in October. There's also a garden you can drift into on warm days.

The Clanfield Tavern, Bampton Road, Clanfield, Bampton, OX18 2RG
Head-cracking timbers, stone-flagged floors and huge log fires at this

15th-century village inn not far from the Thames. Add deep sofas and colourful canvases and you have a civilised place in which to relax with the papers. Owner Tom is passionate about produce, shoots the pheasant, grows the vegetables (beyond the pub garden) and the lamb is reared next door. Set lunches are great value.

The Bell at Sapperton, Sapperton, Cirencester, GL7 6LE

An elegant pub that attracts wine lovers, foodies, ramblers and riders. A spacious but intimate décor spreads itself across several levels, specials are chalked up above the fireplace and the food is generous in its range. Sunday roasts are hugely popular, the well-tended terrace spills into the 'Mediterranean' courtyard, and the wine list matches the clientele.

Photo: The Swan at Southrop, www.theswanatsouthrop.co.uk

Sawday's Travel Club membership opens up hundreds of discounts, treats and other offers in selected B&Bs and hotels in Britain and Ireland, as well as discounts on Sawday's books and other goodies.

Alastair **Sawday's**

TRAVEL CLUB

Here is a little taster of some member offers available at participating special places*:

- 3 nights for the price of 2
- 25% off room price
- Bottle of champagne on arrival
- Late check-out
- Locally produced chocolates
- Organic Dorset cream tea
- Bottle of wine with dinner
- Trout fishing day on the Tamar
- Cornish pasties and Devonshire chutney on arrival
- Free picnic and maps for walkers

To see membership extras and to register visit:

www.sawdays.co.uk/members

Only £25 per year

Sawday's Gift Cards

Sawday's Gift Cards can be used at a whole array of bed and breakfasts, hotels and pubs with rooms scattered across the British Isles. You may fancy a night in a country house which towers majestically over the River Usk, or perhaps a weekend in a splendid Georgian mansion in the Cotswolds. Stay in a garret above a legendary London coffee house or sample a stunning barn conversion in the depths of Northumberland.

Wherever you choose as a treat for yourself, friends or a loved one we know it will be fun, unusual, maybe even eccentric and definitely life affirming. A perfect present.

They come in four denominations – £25, £50, £75 and £100 – and in attractive packaging that includes a series of postcards and a printed booklet featuring all the participating places.

You can purchase Gift Cards at: www.sawdays.co.uk/gift-cards/ or you can order them by phone: +44(0)1275 395431

You can also view the full list of participating places on our website www.sawdays.co.uk and search by this symbol 🎁

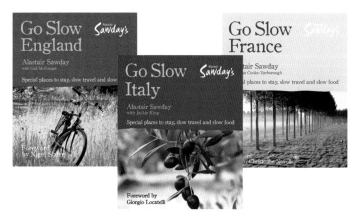

Special places to stay, slow travel and slow food

The Slow Food revolution is upon us and these guides celebrate the Slow philosophy of life with a terrific selection of the places, recipes and people who take their time to enjoy life at its most enriching. In these beautiful books that go beyond the mere 'glossy', you will discover an unusual emphasis on the people who live in Special Slow Places and what they do. Meet farmers, literary people, wine-makers and craftsmen – all with rich stories to tell. *Go Slow England, Go Slow Italy* and our new title *Go Slow France* celebrate fascinating people, fine architecture, history, landscape and real food

"*Go Slow England* is a magnificent guidebook" *BBC Good Food Magazine*

RRP £19.99. To order any of these titles at the Readers' Discount price of £13.00 (plus p&tp) call +44(0)1275 395431 and quote 'Reader Discount COT.

Have you enjoyed this book? Why not try one of the others in the Special Places series and get 35% discount on the RRP *

British Bed & Breakfast (Ed 14)	RRP £14.99	Offer price £9.74
British Bed & Breakfast for Garden Lovers (Ed 5)	RRP £14.99	Offer price £9.74
British Hotels & Inns (Ed 11)	RRP £14.99	Offer price £9.74
Devon & Cornwall (Ed 1)	RRP £ 9.99	Offer price £6.49
Scotland (Ed 1)	RRP £ 9.99	Offer price £6.49
Wales (Ed 1)	RRP £ 9.99	Offer price £6.49
Pubs & Inns of England & Wales (Ed 7)	RRP £15.99	Offer price £10.39
Ireland (Ed 7)	RRP £12.99	Offer price £8.44
French Bed & Breakfast (Ed 11)	RRP £15.99	Offer price £10.39
French Holiday Homes (Ed 5)	RRP £14.99	Offer price £9.74
French Châteaux & Hotels (Ed 6)	RRP £14.99	Offer price £9.74
French Vineyards (Ed 1)	RRP £19.99	Offer price £12.99
Italy (Ed 6)	RRP £14.99	Offer price £9.74
Spain (Ed 8)	RRP £14.99	Offer price £9.74
Portugal (Ed 4)	RRP £11.99	Offer price £7.79
Morocco (Ed 3)	RRP £ 9.99	Offer price £6.49
India & Sri Lanka (Ed 3)	RRP £11.99	Offer price £7.79
Green Europe (Ed 1)	RRP £11.99	Offer price £7.79
Go Slow England (Ed 1)	RRP £19.99	Offer price £12.99
Go Slow Italy (Ed 1)	RRP £19.99	Offer price £12.99
Go Slow France (Ed 1)	RRP £19.99	Offer price £12.99

*postage and packing is added to each order

To order at the Reader's Discount price simply phone
+44 (0)1275 395431 and quote 'Reader Discount COT'.

If you have any comments on entries in this guide, please tell us. If you have a favourite place or a new discovery, please let us know about it. You can return this form to COT, Sawday's, The Old Farmyard, Yanley Lane, Long Ashton, Bristol BS41 9LR, UK or visit www.sawdays.co.uk.

Existing entry

Property name: _____

Entry number: _____ Date of visit: _____

New recommendation

Property name: _____

Address: _____

Tel/Email/Website: _____

Your comments

What did you like (or dislike) about this place? Were the people friendly? What was the location like? What sort of food did they serve?

_____

_____

_____

Your details

Name: _____

Address: _____

_____ Postcode: _____

Tel: _____ Email: _____

Climate Change Our Warming World RRP £12.99 Offer price £8.44

"Climate Change presents in a clear and unique way the greatest challenge facing humanity. It is illustrated with telling photography and sharply written text. It is both objective and passionate. To read it is to know that urgent action is needed at every level in all societies." *Jonathan Dimbleby*

Climate Change is the greatest challenge facing humanity today. In the coming decade a tipping point may be reached triggering irreversible impacts to our planet. This book is not just for scientists or academics, it is for everyone concerned about the future of the earth.

Also available in the Fragile Earth series:
What About China? RRP £6.99 Offer Price £4.54
Ban the Plastic Bag RRP £4.99 Offer Price £3.24
One Planet Living RRP £4.99 Offer Price £3.24
The Little Food Book RRP £8.99 Offer Price £4.54

Visit www.sawdays/bookshop to receive your discount.
Postage & packing are added to each order.

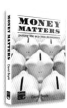

Money Matters
Putting the eco into economics
RRP £7.99 Offer price £5.19

This well-timed book will make you look at everything from your bank statements to the coins in your pocket in a whole new way. Author David Boyle sheds new light on our money system and exposes the inequality, greed and instability of the economies that dominate the world's wealth.

Do Humans Dream of Electric Cars
RRP £4.99 Offer price £3.24

This guide provides a no-nonsense approach to sustainable travel and outlines the simple steps needed to achieve a low carbon future. It highlights innovative and imaginative schemes that are already working, such as car clubs and bike sharing.

The Big Earth Book
Updated paperback edition
RRP £12.99 Offer price 8.44

This book explores environmental, economic and social ideas to save our planet. It helps us understand what is happening to the planet today, exposes the actions of corporations and the lack of action of governments, weighs up new technologies, and champions innovative and viable solutions.

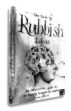

The Book of Rubbish Ideas
RRP £6.99 Offer price £4.54

Every householder should have a copy of this guide to reducing household waste and stopping wasteful behaviour. Containing step-by-step projects, the book takes a top-down guided tour through the average family home.

Alastair
Sawday's
British self-catering

A whole week self-catering in Britain with your friends or family is precious, and you dare not get it wrong. To whom do you turn for advice and who on earth do you trust when the web is awash with advice from strangers? We launched Special Escapes to satisfy an obvious need for impartial and trustworthy help – and that is what it provides. The criteria for inclusion are the same as for our books: we have to like the place and the owners. It has, quite simply, to be 'special'. The site, our first online-only publication, is featured on www.thegoodwebguide.com and is growing fast.

Cosy cottages • Manor houses

Tipis • Hilltop bothies

City apartments and more

www.special-escapes.co.uk

Photo: www.istock.co.uk

① Oxfordshire

② Hotel

③ Old Parsonage Hotel

④ A country house in the city, with a friendly bar for a drop of champagne, a rooftop terrace for afternoon tea and a hidden garden where you can listen to the bells of St Giles. Logs smoulder in the original stone fireplace, the daily papers wait by an ancient window and exquisite art hangs on the walls. You feast in the restaurant on meat from the owner's Oxfordshire farm, then retire to warm stylish bedrooms which are scattered all over the place – some at the front, others in a sympathetic extension. Historical walking tours are 'on the house', while the hotel owns a punt on the Cherwell and will pack you a picnic. Brilliant.

Price	£150–£225. Suites £250.
Rooms	31: 22 twins/doubles, 7 suites for 3, 1 for 4.
Meals	Breakfast £12–£14. Lunch & dinner £10–£45.
Closed	Never.
Directions	From A40 ring road, south onto Banbury Road thro' Summertown. Hotel on right just before St Giles Church.

⑤ ⑥ ⑦ ⑧ ⑨

⑩   ♿ ⛄ 📖 🚒 🚲 📶

⑪ Entry 71 Map 2

Deniz Bostanci
1 Banbury Road, Oxford OX2 6NN
Tel   +44 (0)1865 310210
Web   www.oldparsonage-hotel.co.uk